Developing Soccer Players: Forward-Specific Practices

Dan Bolas

DARK
RIVER

Published in 2018 by Dark River, an imprint of Bennion Kearny Limited.
Copyright © Dark River

ISBN: 978-1-911121-57-2

Published by Dark River, an imprint of Bennion Kearny Limited
6 Woodside
Churnet View Road
Oakamoor
ST10 3AE

To my Dad, Eddie Bolas,
the greatest goal scorer
I never saw play!

About the Author

Dan Bolas started working as a volunteer football coach as part of a community sports leadership award, and immediately got bitten by the coaching bug. Leaving school, he started off working as a community school coach, before moving through the ranks into full-time employment in academy football. He has worked across all levels of the game, ranging from 4 and 5-year olds kicking their first football right through coaching to open age, men's amateur, and semi-professional sides. Dan holds the UEFA A Licence and is a graduate of Premier League's Elite Coach Apprenticeship Scheme.

Table of Contents

Introduction

No matter what level you coach or manage at, one thing will be consistent – the importance of scoring goals. Whilst good defensive organisation and a clear game plan can be massively beneficial to a group's success; it is the ability and consistency of the forward players that will dictate how far a team can go.

In a generation of showboaters, freestylers, and highlight-reel players, the value of a 'good goal scorer' is as important as ever. Someone to finish the creative moves, head home the great crosses, and tap in the winding runs, adds value to the players around them; they provide a focal point for attacking play.

The concept for this book was born out of personal experience. Like many coaches, I am fortunate to watch a lot of football, both televised and live in stadiums. Whilst the main spectacle is always the match, I am intrigued to watch how teams prepare for games – the pre-match 'warm up' activities they do and the rationale behind them (be it technical, tactical, or physical). One of the most common practices is a session where the coach lines up four or five forward players, five metres outside the penalty area, and the forward players take it in turns to play a one-two before shooting at goal from around the edge of the area. It is a practice that everyone will have seen take place, and one that will no doubt continue to be run for years to come.

The problem that this practice creates is that a lot of coaches, further down the football pyramid, believe it to be a realistic and relevant session for the development of forward players. As a 'shooting' practice, some coaches believe that this exercise will give their players the tools they need to develop their finishing skills and this will, in turn, transfer into the game. Unfortunately, this is rarely the case. Even worse, a lot of coaches will copy the session with their own players, believing it will give their forwards enough practice to improve finishing in game scenarios.

The research and practices in this book are designed to help develop the knowledge of coaches working across the football pyramid. Whether it is as an assistant U8 coach who can take a few players during a training session to help develop their ball striking, or someone working with a semi-professional team employing a 'forward specialist' coach to help with their promotion push, the practices you will find here are easy to set up, simple to run, and – most importantly – relevant to the development of forward players!

I hope you find these practices useful, and the information gathered beneficial for your own practice designs in developing forward players.

Dan

"You never get fed up
of scoring goals."
Alan Shearer

Notes

The research in this book has been conducted personally by Dan Bolas. This includes mapping finishes by observing matches using video footage. This has been cross-referenced with data collected by OPTA to confirm accuracy. Information was accurate up to July 2018.

The statistics collected in this book have been taken from elite, professional footballers competing in the top European and World leagues and cups. As a result, players should not be used as direct comparisons, especially when working with younger players or those in a development program. Instead, they are to be used as a guide for helping to develop good practice and habits.

The terminology in this book is designed to be as clear and simple as possible, catering to a wide audience. There may be some words or phrases that may be less common and, whenever possible, these have been explained in a couple of different ways to help with clarity.

In this book, the term 'forward' has been given to a player or players who play in central areas in the attacking third of the pitch. Other terms that may be used commonly include striker, number 9, or centre-forward.

There are occasions when the book may refer to the second six-yard box as a point of reference either as an area to cross/pass the ball into, or a position for the forward to stand. This area refers to the space between the edge of the first six-yard box and the penalty spot. It is the same width as the first six-yard box. Whilst not marked on a field, it is a good visual reference when working with forward players.

This book focuses on finishing and is not a comprehensive guide to all-round forward play. There are numerous aspects to the modern day forward that are required in order to be successful; this is just one part of their game.

Technique-Based Practices

It is well documented that some of the most technically elite footballers from the past 30 years honed their craft by practicing alone. The repetition of technique allows for the individual to 'feel' what works well for them and, with the absence of pressure or opposition, there is a freedom to explore, experiment, and refine.

Whilst researching and identifying the finishing requirements of forwards within football, a number of techniques constantly appeared. Be they in children's small-sided football, right through to the FIFA World Cup, these techniques seemed both frequent and successful, making them a key part of any forward player's 'toolkit'.

The identified techniques were

- Striking the ball with the laces

- Striking the ball with the inside of the foot

- Toe poking the ball past the goalkeeper

- Volleying the ball

- Chipping the ball over a standing goalkeeper

- Dinking the ball over a grounded goalkeeper

- Rounding the goalkeeper

- Heading the ball with power from a floated cross

- Heading the ball with a flicked touch from a firm / quick cross

- An adaptive finish using a creative technique (for example an overhead kick or back heel)

Building from this, the following pages highlight simple, easy to set up practices which allow forwards to practice these techniques, either alone or with a coach, in order to enhance their skills and proficiency.

Each session has a number of 'balls' required in order to complete one repetition. This is ideal for when a forward is working alone and can practice five or six times before collecting the balls and working from the opposite side with a different angle. Intensity in these sessions should also be low, meaning that between goes, the forward should be walking back to the start position, and maintaining a relatively low heart rate. This allows the player to fully focus on the technique aspect of the practice.

These practices could be used as homework for young forwards, or an arrival activity for players who get to training earlier than others. There is also the option to use these sessions as cool down activities for some players, as a way of ending training; even for those who stay behind once the rest of the team have gone.

As with all ball striking activity, there a couple of key points to remember. Firstly, striking a football over longer distances or with considerable power places stress on the muscles, in particular the quadriceps and calf muscles. Raising the leg to volley, or reaching to toe poke the ball, will also engage the groin muscles. Activating these muscles (through a warm-up) prior to ball striking is highly recommended by many sports scientists, physiotherapists, and strength and conditioning coaches. The value of a meaningful warm-up should, therefore, be taken into account before starting any sort of practice of this nature.

Secondly, ball striking repetition does carry a risk of overuse injury. Doing large numbers of the same movement with any muscle group is not recommended. Therefore, mixing up the technical sessions would be considered best practice.

The practices here can (and should) be adapted and evolved to suit the needs of individual players, and forwards should be encouraged to change start positions and distances in order to develop their technique from different angles and areas.

“Everything is practice.”
Pele

Psychology

In modern football, sport psychology is a big part of any first team set up or development program. Players from all levels are challenged to think about their behaviours and how they affect their performances, identifying positive traits that may give them a competitive edge on the pitch. Even before it was 'formalised' within football, forward players have been reliant on their 'mindset' to be successful, both in how they practice and how they perform. The demands placed upon those 'responsible for scoring the goals' is high, and some of the best forwards of all time have paid testament to their mental strengths.

Focussing purely on the goalscoring aspect of forward play, there are a number of considerations a coach should take into account when working with forward players in order to help develop the mental skills required to play the position. Whilst the coach may not be a trained psychologist, these tips may provide the forward with an advantage in addition to the technical detail they are receiving.

Calm and composed. The best finishers look relaxed when they are striking the ball into the net. Players such as Harry Kane and Sergio Agüero do things very quickly in and around the penalty box, but at the point of striking the football, they seem calm and controlled in their actions. Creating a practice environment in which the forward becomes calm and composed – irrespective of what is going on around them – is a good place to start when working with a forward player.

COACH'S TIP - The tempo and volume of the coach's voice can create a level for the forward to work from. Shouting and talking quickly causes the player to feel pressure and become rushed. Use a controlled, clear tone that allows the forward to relax.

Reset and focus. Forwards will miss chances. It is part of football, and even elite forwards will have a shot-to-goal ratio between 15 and 30% over the course of a season. With this in mind, consider the type of practices the coach should do with the forward player; they should treat each shot as an individual strike, and not dwell on a miss or overpraise a finish. This will allow the forward to get used to resetting after each chance, and providing the next finish with the same care and attention.

COACH'S TIP - Limit praise or technical correction to a few short words between finishes, allowing the forward to take the information on board and clear their head for the next one. Avoid language such as 'Remember when you missed...' or 'That's two poor finishes in a row' as this will create a mindset of negative thinking, replaying back poor practice in the head.

Positivity and self-belief. Believing that a finish will be a goal is a key part of any forward's mindset. Negative thoughts just prior to striking the ball can only damage the forward's technique, as they start to second guess and adapt to what their instinct is telling them. This is not to say every session should be 'over the top' positive, as praising poor finishing is not beneficial at all. It is simply a case of finding a way of delivering information to the forward player in a way that instils self-belief and confidence. This will transfer onto the field of play.

COACH'S TIP - The language used by the coach is key here. Avoid words such as *try* and *attempt*, instead focus on words such as *score* and *finish*. When a finish is missed, or a forward is finding a particular technique difficult, use questions to ask where they feel they are going wrong. Then guide them towards the 'correct' answer if they don't get there by themselves.

Have high standards. Depending on the level of player the coach is working with, there will be a chance that the forward will demand a high level of performance in their practice. As a coach, meeting this by setting targets will help them develop further. For younger players, or those lower down the football pyramid, finishing sessions should be enjoyable, but at the same time taken seriously, with technique and the practice being beneficial. Encouraging players to work to the best of their ability, as well as emphasising the importance of good practice in these individual sessions, will have a long-term effect on their mindset.

COACH'S TIP - Language and *when* to say things are a key part of developing high standards within sessions. If a player is lacking concentration or deliberately practicing poor technique, raising this with the player is beneficial for all parties. By the same token, if a player is working at their highest level, and missing the goal a lot, it is important to focus on the technique and what they are doing, as opposed to blaming the player.

Make it competitive. One of the hardest aspects of any sort of individual practice is developing a realistic feel. The scenario may be right, and the technique may be correct, but without the pressure of winning or losing, it is difficult to mirror what will go on during a match. Making these sessions competitive, using a scoring system or league table (which rolls over a series of sessions or weeks) will help players remain on task, and gain the feeling that what they are doing 'matters'.

All the above points will help develop a player's mentality towards finishing, with the end focus being in-game improvement. With all this in mind, perhaps the most important point of all when a forward is finding something difficult (perhaps when trying a new technique or working something else) is to focus on the process of the actions they are doing. Be it head position, ball contact, or movement – breaking things down and looking at the 'issue' in smaller chunks will help increase self-belief and ultimately improve performance. The language the coach uses here also has a part to play. If the coach uses closed praise such as 'Good Goal' or 'Nice Header', they are focusing on the end result, not the process. The same finish could be praised with 'Well done for heading the ball downwards'; this would allow the forward to focus on the technique (emphasising the process) and give them something to take on for future practice.

"For me, soccer provides so many emotions, a different feeling every day."
Ronaldinho

Statistics and Best Practice

Over the following pages, there is a collection of data from some of the top forward players across Europe. This data has been compiled in order to give context to the types of finishing present in the European and International game over recent seasons, with the ultimate focus being on how to develop and improve players to be ready for the challenges that they may face on match day.

The information looks at five of the top centre forwards across the top European leagues, Harry Kane, Mauro Icardi, Robert Lewandowski, Luis Suárez and Radamel Falcao. We also look at the goalscoring record of Miroslav Klose, the leading goalscorer in World Cup football. The finishing maps are designed to show developing footballers the positions in which these top forwards score their goals, which may affect their positioning in training sessions and, most importantly, games.

Then, we follow up with statistics regarding the number of touches per goal, average number of shots per match, and average minutes played per match; data which can again be used to influence when and how the coach delivers their forward-specific sessions.

It has already been mentioned how it is important to remember that this information should be used to help design game-realistic practices, and not used as a direct comparison, especially when working with young and developing players. Players playing mini soccer will naturally have more opportunities to score goals, and depending on the level and standard of the game in which the player is playing, numbers can be drastically different.

All data has been cross-referenced with OPTA.

Harry Kane

League: English Premier League

Club: Tottenham Hotspur

Season: 2017/18

Primary Formation(s) Used:
4-2-3-1 / 3-4-2-1

Games Played: 37

Goals Scored:
30 Total
13 Right Foot
10 Left Foot
6 Headers
1 Other

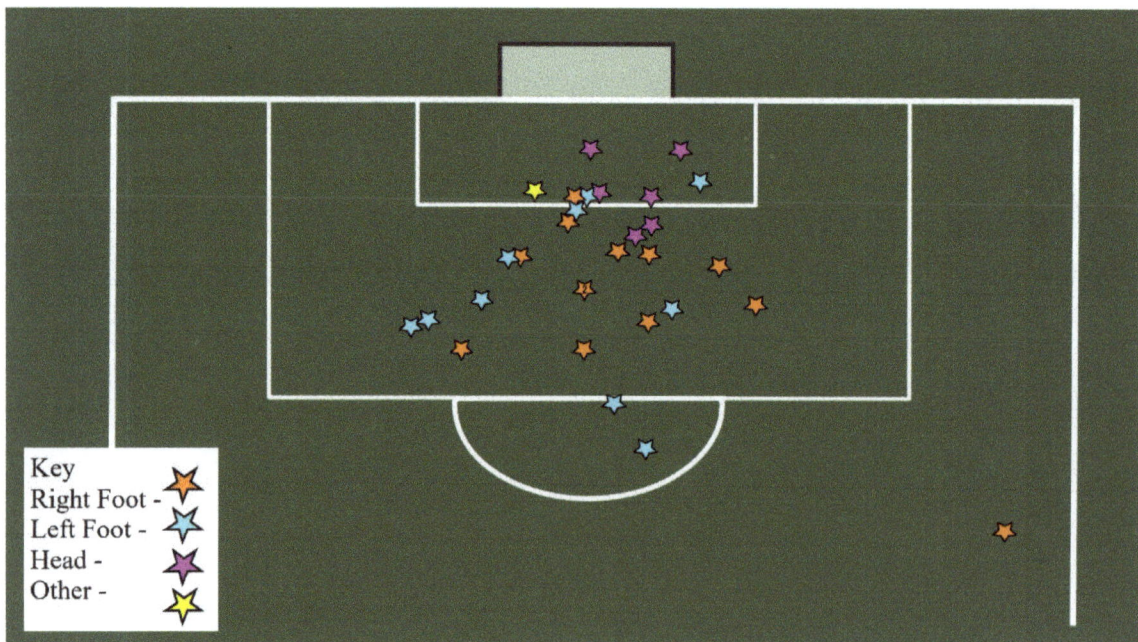

Key
Right Foot -
Left Foot -
Head -
Other -

Analysis

Playing as a lone forward, Kane was often the focal point for Tottenham's attacking play. His map shows he is able to finish from a range of angles in the penalty area and is able to do so comfortably with both feet, displaying technical excellence. The majority of his goals fall within the second six-yard box area.

Luis Suárez

League: Spanish La Liga

Club: FC Barcelona

Season: 2017/18

Primary Formation(s) Used:
4-4-2

Games Played: 33

Goals Scored:
25 Total
19 Right Foot
4 Left Foot
2 Headers
0 Other

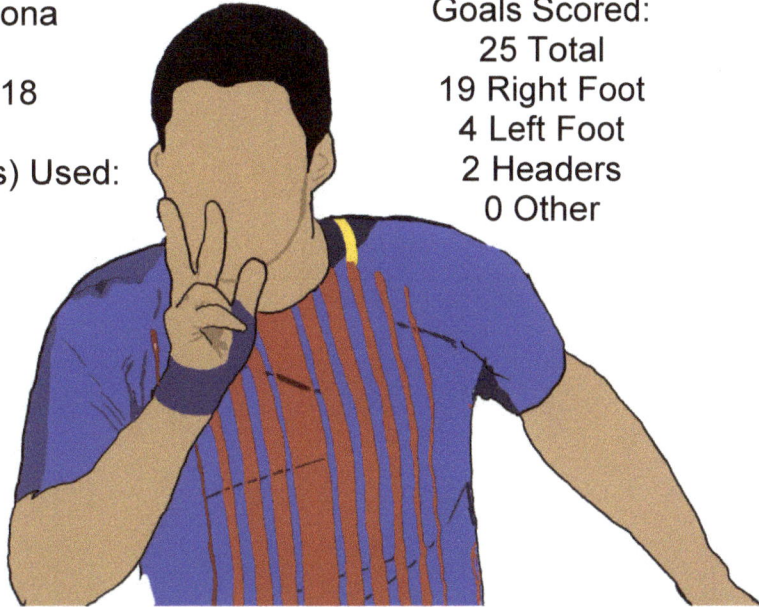

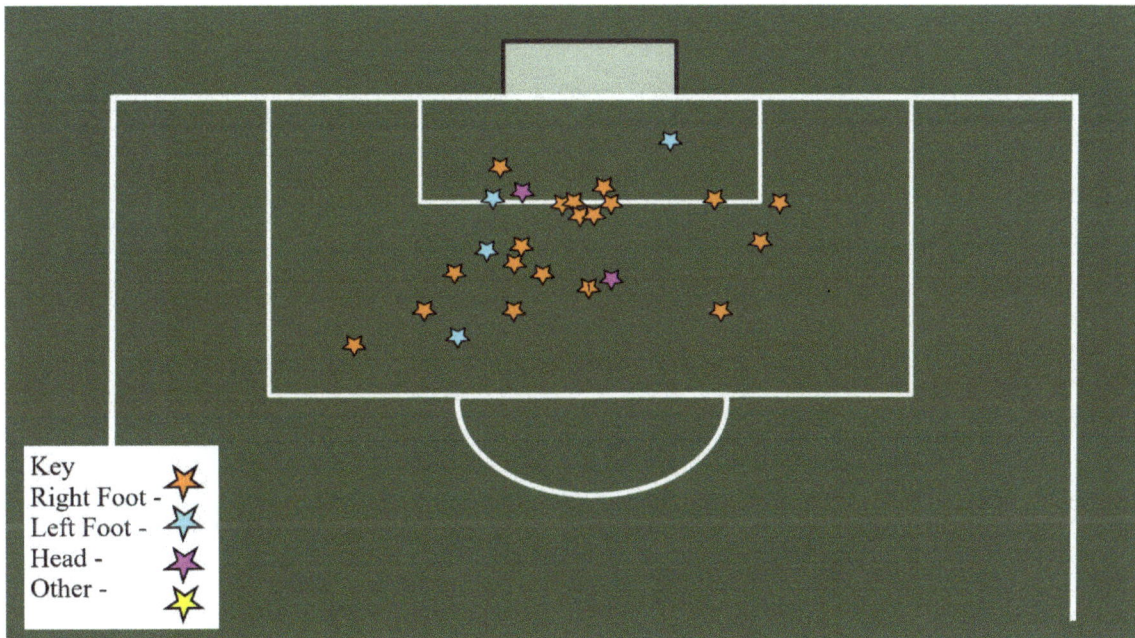

Key
Right Foot -
Left Foot -
Head -
Other -

Analysis

Playing alongside Lionel Messi, Suarez's movement off the ball and aggression to attack the ball in the penalty area results in many of his goals, especially on the edge of the six-yard box (10). Suarez is comfortable shooting early, which is why a number of his goals come from wider angles. Notice he did not score this season from outside the penalty area.

Mauro Icardi

League: Italian Serie A

Club: Internazionale

Season: 2016/17

Primary Formation(s) Used:
4-2-3-1/4-3-1-2

Games Played: 34

Goals Scored:
24 Total
14 Right Foot
3 Left Foot
7 Headers
0 Other

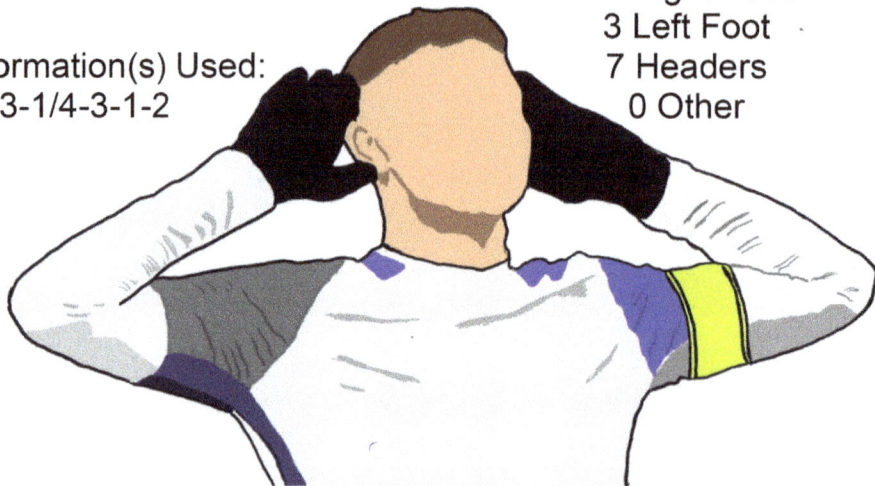

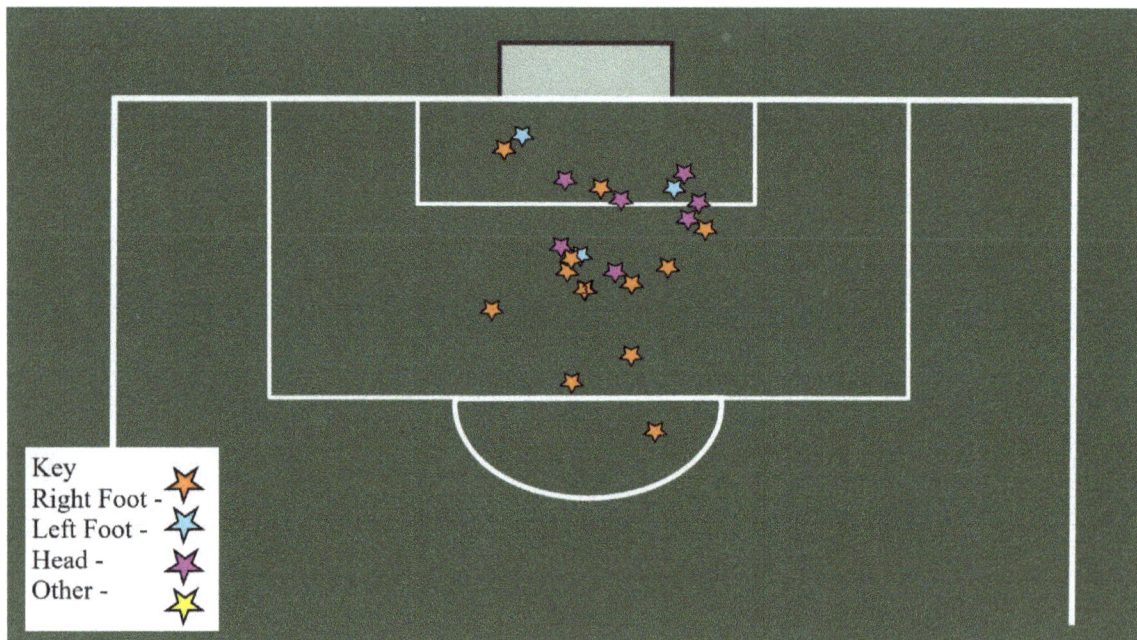

Key
Right Foot -
Left Foot -
Head -
Other -

Analysis

A creative finisher, Mauro Icardi has garnered a reputation for being able to score using both controlled and unorthodox techniques. Nearly a third of his goals in the 2016/17 season were headers, either directly from crosses, or reactive rebounds to an initial shot. Very good at getting in-between defenders and being difficult to mark.

Miroslav Klose

Competition: FIFA World Cup

Nation: Germany

Years: 2002 / 2006 / 2010 / 2014

Primary Formation(s) Used:
3-4-1-2 /4-2-3-1

Games Played: 24

Goals Scored:
16 Total
8 Right Foot
1 Left Foot
7 Headers
0 Other

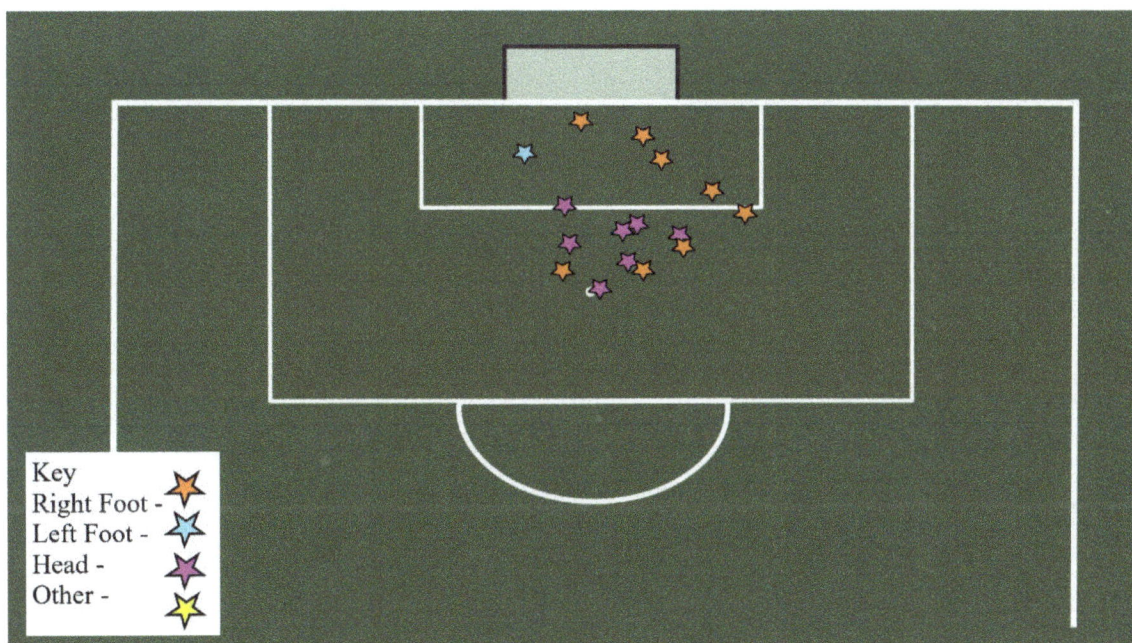

Key
Right Foot -
Left Foot -
Head -
Other -

Analysis

The record holder for World Cup goals, Klose adapted his style of play to move with the changing tactics of the German national team. The majority of his headed goals came in 2002 when more direct crossed balls were being played. All goals were scored in the first and second six-yard box areas, with 14 of the 16 being one-touch finishes.

Radamel Falcao

League: French Ligue 1

Club: AS Monaco

Season: 2016/17

Primary Formation(s) Used:
4-4-2

Games Played: 29

Goals Scored:
21 Total
14 Right Foot
3 Left Foot
4 Headers
0 Other

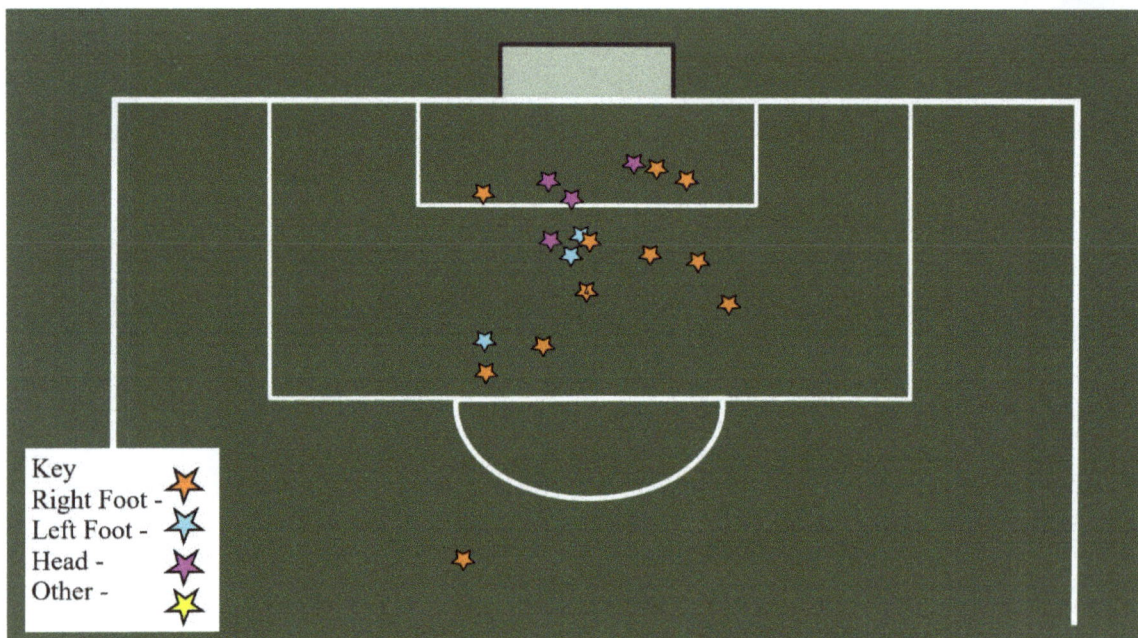

Key
Right Foot -
Left Foot -
Head -
Other -

Analysis

Falcao acted as the finisher for a Ligue 1 winning side in the 2016/17 season, playing alongside some young, creative players that possessed pace and guile. Twenty of his goals came inside the area, all finished within the width of the six-yard box, highlighting his positioning. Falcao also is able to manipulate the ball quickly in order to strike with his right foot.

Robert Lewandowski

League: German Bundesliga

Club: Bayern Munich

Season: 2017/18

Primary Formation(s) Used:
4-3-3 / 4-2-3-1

Games Played: 30

Goals Scored:
29 Total
18 Right Foot
6 Left Foot
5 Headers
0 Other

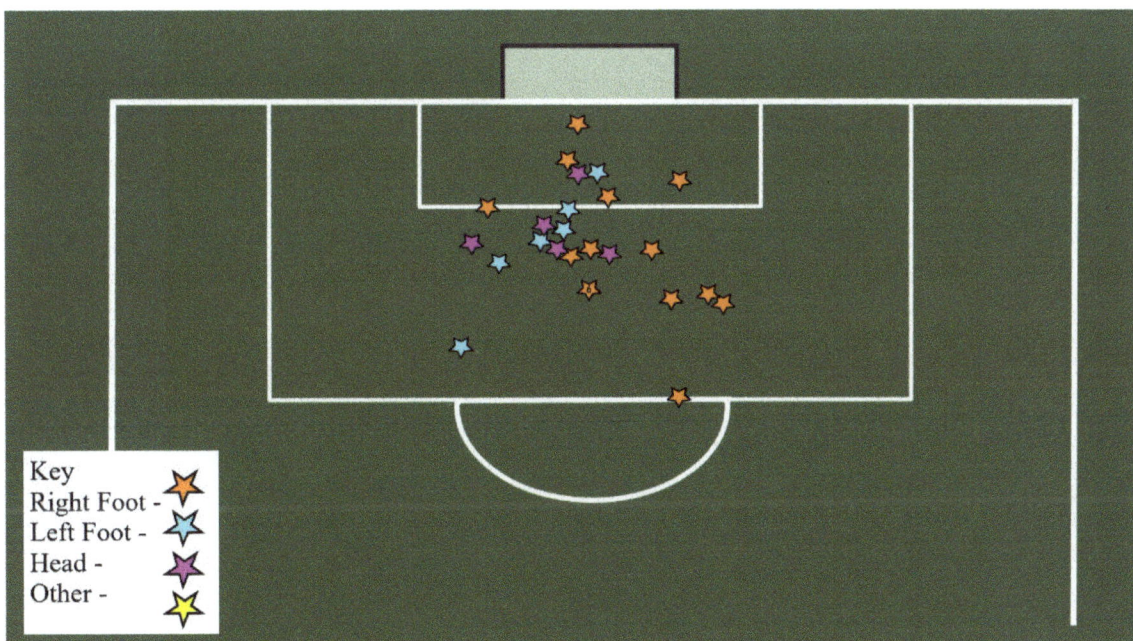

Key
Right Foot -
Left Foot -
Head -
Other -

Analysis

Averaging nearly a goal a game, Lewandowski's ability to finish with both feet and his head highlights his value to his team. Playing with two wide players, it is no surprise that 27 of his goals are finished within the first and second six-yard boxes, with both crosses and combination play being strong supply sources.

Goals, Shots, and Touches

Table 1 shows the number of touches taken by ten of Europe's top forwards when scoring their final ten goals of the 2017/18 domestic season.

Touches Per Goal

	One Touch	Two Touches	Three Touches	Four Touches	Five +	
Kane	7	1	2			
Lukaku	5	2	1	1	1	
Aguero	3	4	3			
Cavani	7	3				
Lewandowski	9	1				
Suarez	8	2				
Immobile	6	2	1		1	
Higuain	5		4		1	
Griezmann	5	2		3		
Icardi	7	2			1	
Total	62	19	11	4	4	100

Last 10 Goals of 2017/18 Season

Table 2 highlights the average number of shots and minutes played for the same ten forwards throughout the entire 2017/18 domestic season.

Average Shots & Time per Game

	Average Shots per 90 Minutes	Average Match time (minutes)
Kane	5.32	84
Lukaku	2.7	84
Aguero	4.31	79
Cavani	3.68	81
Lewandowski	5.28	72
Suarez	3.75	88
Immobile	3.66	82
Higuain	3.27	80
Griezmann	2.58	79
Icardi	2.96	88
	37.51	817
Total	3.751	81.7

The following pie chart is linked to Table 1 to show a visual breakdown of the % of goals scored with the number of touches taken.

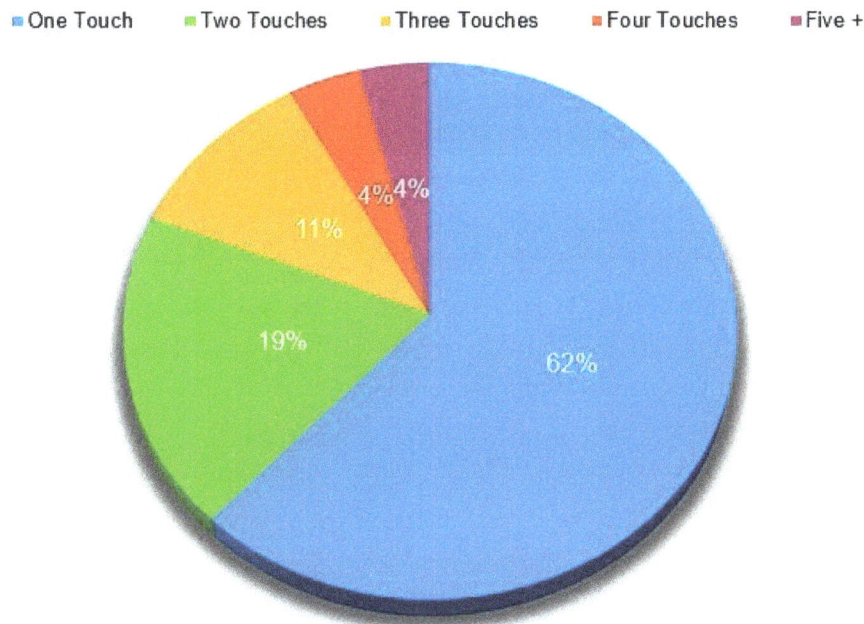

Considerations for Practice

In order to prepare players for the demands of football, sessions should give individuals and groups the opportunity to practice the techniques required to succeed in game-realistic situations.

The statistical information over the previous pages should provide coaches and managers with key points that will influence their practice design, both in whole group sessions and specifically when working with forwards.

When designing sessions that involve finishing, the below points should also be considered.

Number of touches. With 62% of finishes from top European forwards being first time, developing practices that challenge the forward to shoot with one touch is important. The variety in one touch finishing could be from crosses, rebounds, or from a simple set pass; however, the technique of judging the flight, pace, and spin on the ball (in order to make a clean connection) is an important part of a forward's 'toolkit', and should be practiced.

Use both feet. Of the 145 goals scored by the highlighted forwards, just 18.6% were scored with the player's non-preferred foot. Harry Kane was the exception to this, netting 33% of his goals with his left boot. The ability to finish using both feet is most definitely beneficial, and should therefore be practiced. However, top forwards often find a way of positioning their body in order to score with their preferred foot, and coach's should be aware of this when working with forward players.

Heading the ball. Seven of Klose's 16 World Cup goals were with his head. That statistic alone indicates that, even at the highest level against international defenders, there will be an opportunity to head towards goal. Whilst repetitive heading is not advisable at any age or stage of development, encourage the correct technique with youngsters; honing those skills with clever practice design is a must for developing a forward's all-round finishing.

Style of play. The way in which a team plays has little impact on the types of finish. Nine of Lewandowski's last 10 goals for Bayern Munich were one-touch finishes. Suarez had a similar number (8) with Barcelona. Both these sides have a reputation for dominating the ball and won their domestic leagues comfortably. At the same time, Agüero (3) and Higuain (5) played in equally successful, possession-dominant sides, yet scored a number of their goals with two-four touches. Whilst practice design should be relevant to the style of play, finishing sessions should provide a variety of experiences for forwards.

The second six-yard box. As discussed previously, the 12 yards from the goal line along the width of the six-yard box is a crucial area for forwards to operate. Of the 145 goals scored by the highlighted forwards, just 28 finishes fell outside this area, with two of them being direct free kicks. The statistics show there is a greater chance of forwards scoring within this area and, as a result, practice design should factor this in.

Opposition. With a huge 96% of the goals from the highlighted forwards being finished inside the penalty box, the presence of opposition pressure when taking a shot is both likely and important. At the same time, it is important to remember that few tackles take place inside the penalty box nowadays, with interceptions and blocks being the primary source of defensive influence in the area. Incorporate a sense of pressure, either by limiting space or adding passive, blocking defenders in practice designs.

Number of repetitions. The information about the average number of shots per 90 minutes highlights the need for efficiency in front of goal from top forwards, but also has an impact on the number of times forwards should be practicing a particular technique. Fifty or sixty shots in a training session not only places the player at risk of developing an injury but also isn't realistic to the demands of the game. Consider how many times a forward practices a technique before moving on to a different angle or practice.

Time in the game. The statistics from the top level of European football shows that forwards play, on average, 81.7 minutes per 90 minute match. Therefore putting on forward-specific practices around 65 - 70 minutes into a team training session would provide them with the chance to practice whilst fatigued; something which relates to the scenario they may find themselves in on game day. Depending on the age group coached, and the size of the squad available, most forwards lower down the footballing pyramid will play for the full 90 minutes.

When designing a practice to benefit any forward's finishing ability, the above considerations can act as a starting point for when, where, and how to set up the session. However, it is important to remember these statistics are taken from the top end of the game, and that the age group, ability of the player, and level in which they are competing, should be taken into account.

Penalty Kicks

Penalty kicks are a crucial moment in any game, be it an opportunity to take the lead within 90 minutes, or the pressure of a shootout following a lengthy cup tie. At the higher levels of the game, the responsibility for taking a penalty will usually fall on one of two people, the team's captain or the senior forward.

Developing strong penalty taking technique is an asset to any developing forward, for a number of reasons. As the focal point of attacking play, many coaches or managers will look to their forward to stand up and score a penalty. Often, the forward will have been involved in the build-up to the penalty being awarded, either directly being fouled or indirectly in the passage of play prior. Perhaps most importantly, it is a great opportunity for a forward to add another goal to their scoring record in that season or competition.

Penalty taking is a closed skill. This means that the variables for the technique are minimal. The ball will always be on the penalty spot, the same distance away from the goal on each kick. The only opposition will be a goalkeeper, who will be on their goal line until the ball is struck. The ball will always be still at the point of contact. The taker can always run up to the ball at their preferred pace and angle, and it can be struck however they wish. With this taken into consideration, practicing the technique is both sensible and highly beneficial.

Below are some points that will help forward players with their technique when taking penalties, alongside some advice for coaches on how to develop good habits.

Clear the head. When a penalty is awarded, there is usually some sort of controversy or complaint involved. Opposition players may be protesting the decision, a red card may have been issued, or a clear goalscoring opportunity may have been denied. Opposing players may approach the taker, kick the ball away, or stand in positions that delay the taking of the kick. Here, the key is to get the forward to clear their mind, either focussing on where they are going to put the kick, or simply zoning out of the scenario and ignoring the goings on around them.

Know the best penalty. The best penalty takers have two or three 'stock' penalties that they are comfortable striking when under perceived pressure. These techniques have been practiced and honed for hours on the training field, so when it comes to taking one at a crucial time, they don't need to think about their run-up, body placement, or ball striking, Encourage forward players to have two 'stock' penalties (potentially ones that go in different sides of the goal) in order to develop a confidence in striking the ball.

Hit the target. Perhaps the most simplistic piece of information, however no penalty has ever gone in the goal if it has been struck over the bar or wide of the post! If on target, a poorly struck penalty may wrong-foot the GK or – if the GK goes the right way – it may still go through their hands or under their body. Emphasise the importance of hitting the target at every attempt during practice, in order for it to become habit.

Have a routine. Look at a free throw shooter in basketball, a penalty kicker in rugby, or an Olympic high jumper. Before they take each attempt, many will have a set routine they go through. From stepping out the run-up, to adjusting their socks, these quirks are designed to place the athlete in a familiar state which allows them to complete the technique required. In football, dead ball specialists such as Cristiano Ronaldo, David Beckham, and Roberto Carlos also followed similar routines. Having your forward player go through the same short routine before each penalty helps develop confidence and focus ahead of the ball being struck.

You will score. Perhaps the most important piece of advice is the taker 'knowing' that they will score the penalty kick. The GK, elements of the crowd, and opposing players will be doing everything they can to put the taker off, but having the self-belief that scoring *will be* outcome plays a massive part in the success of any penalty.

A good penalty is one that ends up in the goal. Whether it is struck firmly into the side netting, rolled to the opposite side of where the GK has dived, or passed firmly into the top corner, the desired result is the ball crossing the line and the GK not stopping it. With this said, the following graphic highlights the variety of successful penalty kicks.

Penalty Kick Analysis

Location in which penalties were scored in the group stage of the 2018 World Cup

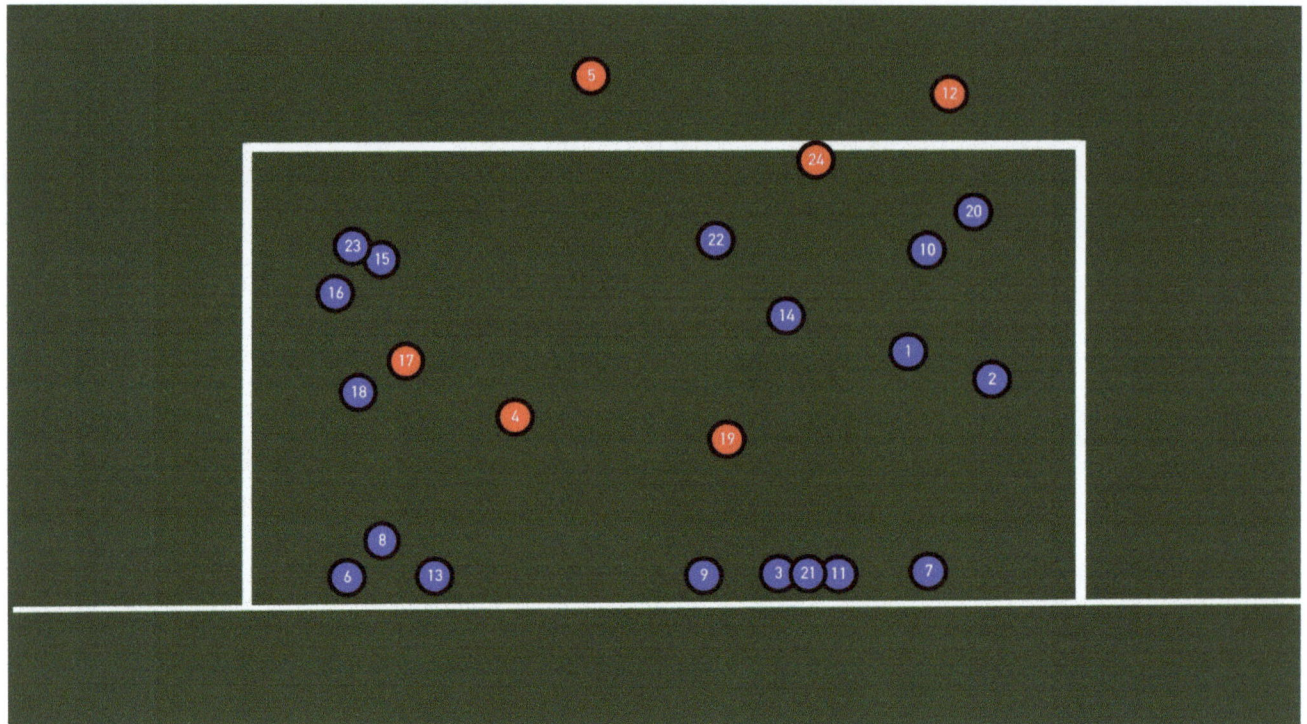

1. Cristiano Ronaldo for Portugal vs Spain
2. Antoine Griezmann for France vs Australia
3. Mile Jedinak for Australia vs France
4. Lionel Messi for Argentina vs Iceland
5. Christian Cueva for Peru vs Denmark
6. Luka Modric for Croatia vs Nigeria
7. Andreas Granqvist for Sweden vs South Korea
8. Ferjani Sassi for Tunisia vs England
9. Shinji Kagawa for Japan vs Colombia
10. Mohamed Salah for Egypt vs Russia
11. Mile Jedinak for Australia vs Denmark
12. Gylfi Sigurðsson for Iceland vs Nigeria
13. Eden Hazard for Belgium vs Tunisia
14. Carlos Vela for Mexico vs South Korea
15. Harry Kane for England vs Panama
16. Harry Kane for England vs Panama
17. Fahad Al Muwallad for Saudi Arabia vs Egypt
18. Fahad Al Muwallad for Saudi Arabia vs Egypt
19. Cristiano Ronaldo for Portugal vs Iran
20. Karim Ansarifard for Iran vs Portugal
21. Victor Moses for Nigeria vs Argentina
22. Gylfi Sigurðsson for Iceland vs Croatia
23. Andreas Granqvist for Sweden vs Mexico
24. Bryan Ruiz for Costa Rica vs Switzerland
(Rebound hit GK and went into goal - own goal given)

From the penalty kicks shown above, there is clearly not a notable pattern about a guaranteed successful penalty. Whether hit high or low, there is a strong chance the ball will end up in the net, with takers striking the ball around stomach height seeing their kicks more likely to be saved.

Kicks that went low were still struck with good force, with a mixed technique of laces and inside of the foot being used.

It is interesting to note that two players seen as the 'the best footballers in the world' both had their kicks saved (with both kicks taking place at key times during the match) highlighting how – irrespective of the technical level of the taker – the pressure of the kick can effect anyone!

Considerations for Practice
When practicing, ensure the taker makes good contact with the ball, either with laces or the inside of the foot. Aim high in top corners or low, avoiding the middle lateral third of the goal. Most importantly, ensure the kick hits the target!

This looks simple...

"Simplicity is Genius," Albert Einstein.

One of the key aspects of developing finishing is to focus on the technique required to be successfully executed under pressure. This can be achieved by placing the forward in a position which they may find themselves in, on the pitch (or a scenario that may occur in the game) and then allowing them to 'practice' the technique, develop a feel for a successful strike, and continue to do this until it becomes 'comfortable'.

The sessions you will find in this book are designed to be simple to set up, simple to repeat, and allow for a number of repetitions in order for forwards to develop the required techniques to become more efficient in front of goal.

Equipment

Depending on the venue you use to run your training sessions, certain items of equipment may or may not be available. Replicating certain items is simple enough. Rebound boards can be replaced with school benches turned on their sides, or failing this, a coach can act as a rebound surface. Using larger cones (for example, traffic-style cones) works, and poles are a cheap and efficient alternative to mannequins.

"You have got to shoot,
otherwise you can't score."
Johan Cruyff

Finishing Technique: Laces

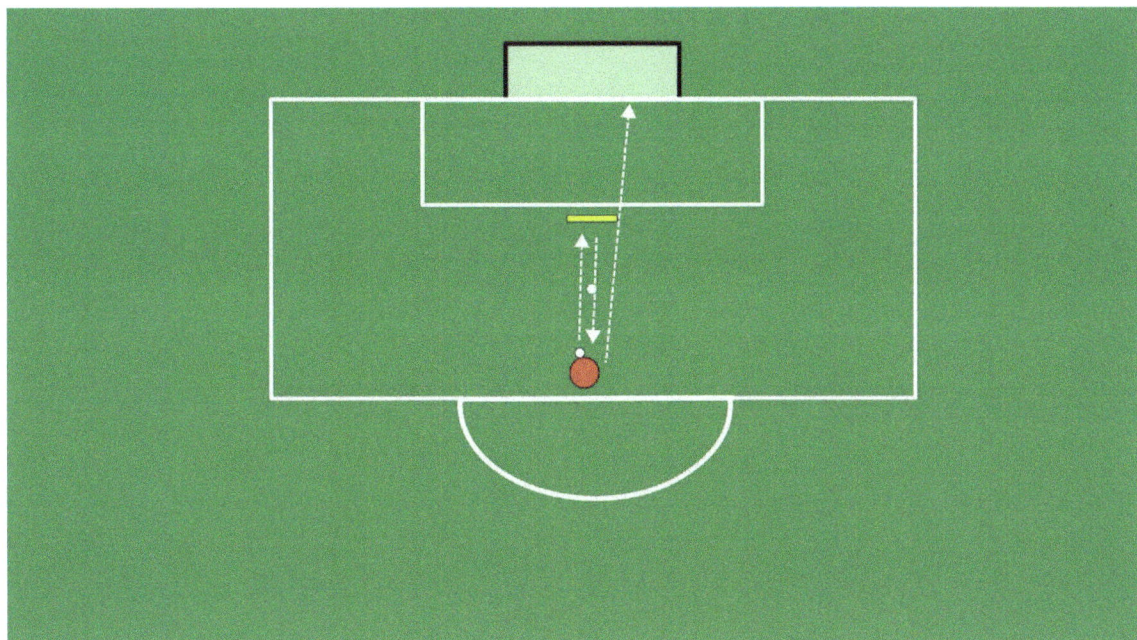

Practice	Key Technical Points
Pass the ball into the rebound board with the inside of the foot. Strike the ball towards goal using your laces. Aim to get the ball either over, or to the side of, the rebound board. After 1 repetition, change the angle and position of the rebound board in order to create a different challenge. Practice striking the ball with both feet. 1 Repetition = 8 Balls.	The forward should be ready to strike the ball as soon as it hits the rebound board, and be able to adapt to the angle and pace the ball comes back towards them. Have bodyweight forwards. This will help with a controlled strike. Keep head over the ball when striking the ball to keep the shot low. Get close to the ball before striking (don't reach).

Best Practice Examples	Coach's Tip
Messi [2018 WC] vs Nigeria Dzagoev [Euro 2012] vs Czech Republic Neymar (2nd goal) [2014 WC] vs Cameroon	Alternate left foot and right foot, striking with the laces in order to become more natural at both.

Finishing Technique: Inside of the Foot

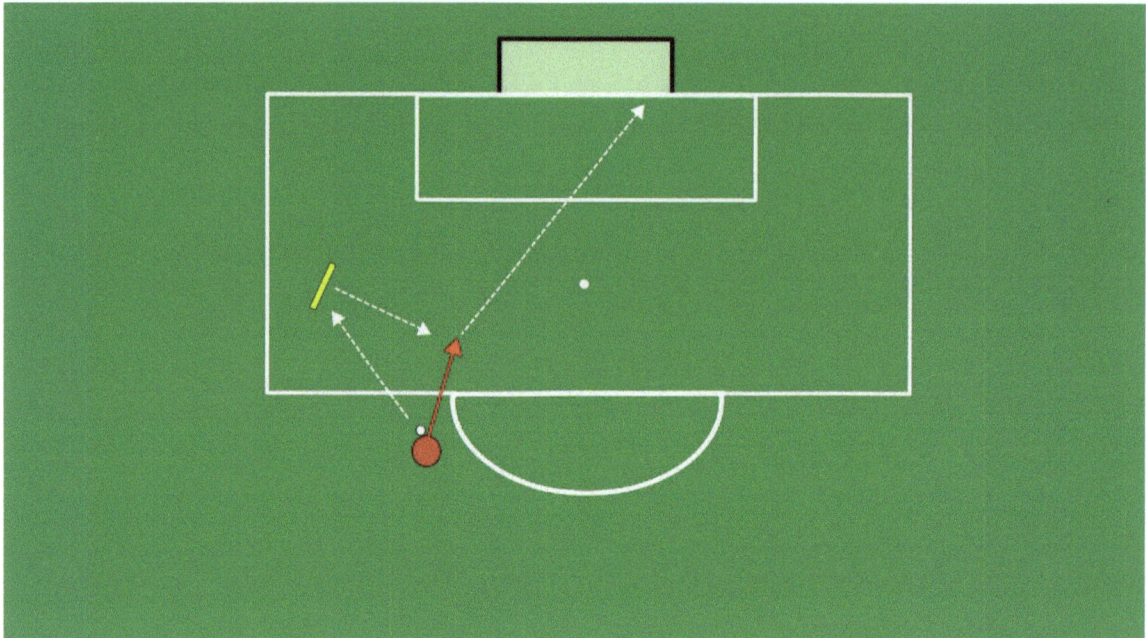

Practice

Forward passes the ball against the rebound board with the inside of the foot.

As the ball comes back, forward lets the ball run across their body and strikes the ball with the inside of the foot (right foot if attacking from the left).

Depending on the rebound, the player may need to take a touch, or take it first time.

Practice from both sides.

1 Repetition = 6 Balls.

Key Technical Points

After the rebound, work body shape so it is open, and chest is pointing towards the goal.

Strike the ball with the inside of the foot, either in the middle for a straighter shot, or on the outside of the ball for a curling shot.

Aim for the opposite inside netting.

Make sure the strike has some pace on it.

Best Practice Examples

Cavani [2018 WC] vs Portugal
Poulsen [2018 WC] vs Peru
Di Natale [Euro 2012] vs Spain

Coach's Tip

Following the rebound, challenge the forward to work at speed to give the technique a realistic feel.

Finishing Technique: Toe Poke

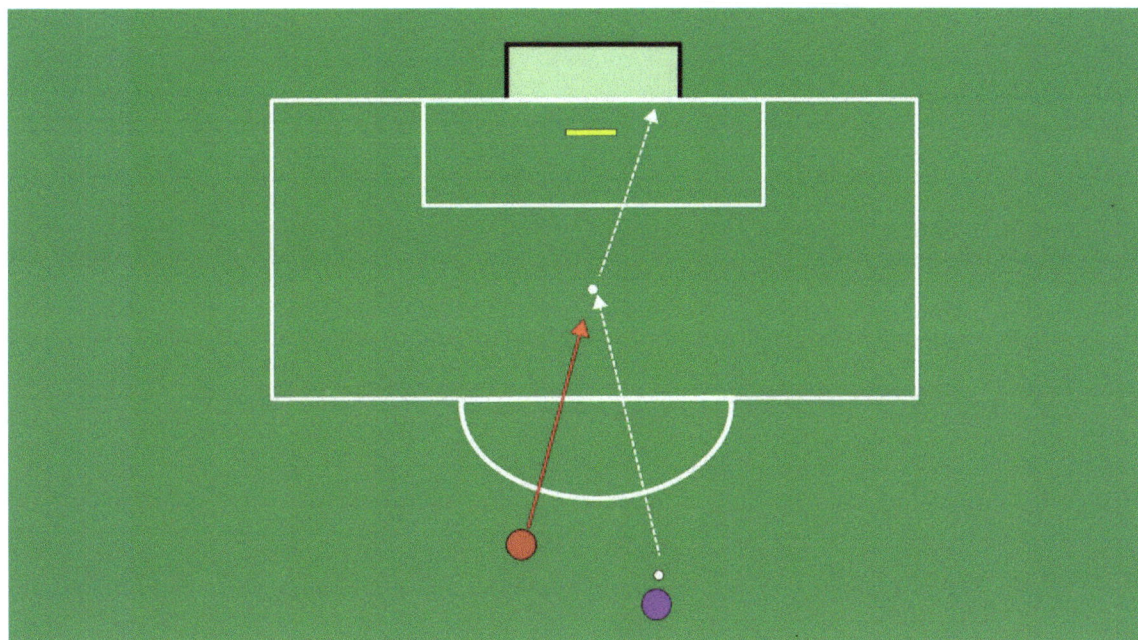

Practice

Coach takes a touch out of their feet and then passes the ball with the inside of the foot towards the penalty spot.

On coach's touch, forward starts to run into the penalty box.

Forward to shoot first time with their toe, poking the ball into the corner of the net.

If the ball hits the rebound board, forward to score first time on the rebound.

1 Repetition = 6 Balls.

Key Technical Points

Pass and forward run to be done at speed.

Strike the ball with the toe, aiming to make contact with the middle of the ball.

Emphasis on using the pace on the through pass to generate the power, changing the direction of the finish.

Stay alert after the initial shot, and ready for a rebound if the ball comes back.

Best Practice Examples

Szalai [Euro 2016] vs Hungary
Griezmann [Euro 2016] vs Germany
Oscar [2014 WC] vs Croatia

Coach's Tip

Encourage the player to take the shot early, as the benefit of this type of finish is the element of surprise. This may mean reaching for the ball.

Finishing Technique: Volley

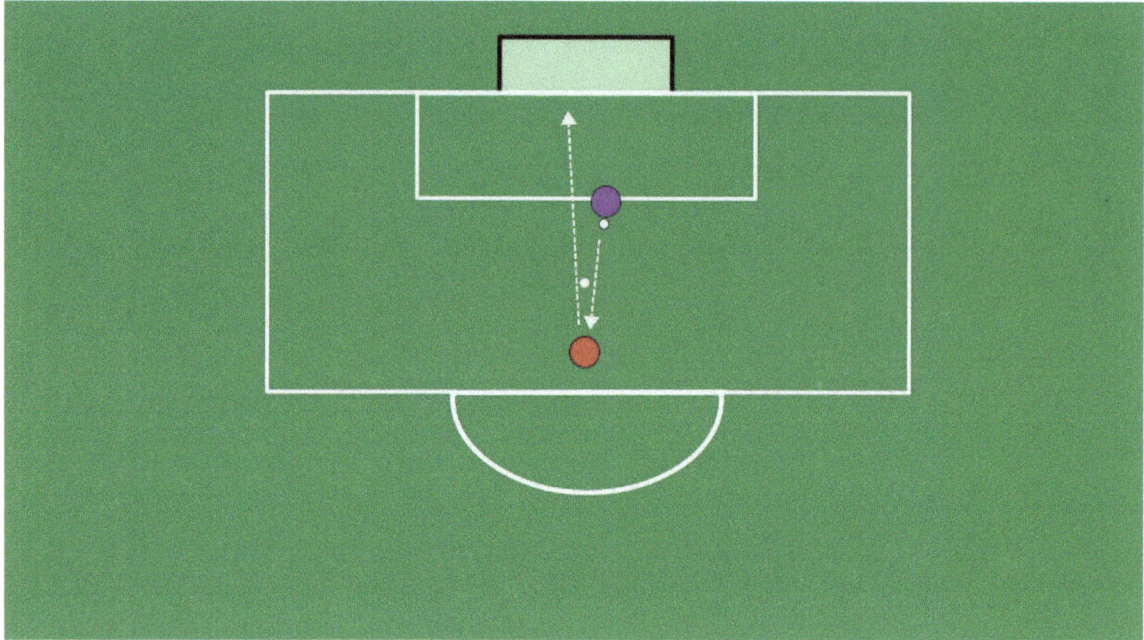

Practice
Coach bounces the ball. The ball is then thrown into the forward with a two-handed, underarm throw. The throw must go no higher than head height, and arrive at the forward between waist and knee. Forward adapts body to the throw and strikes the ball first time into the goal. Coach does not need to throw the ball directly to the forward; it can be served from different sides. 1 Repetition = 6 Balls.

Key Technical Points
Forward must keep their eyes on the ball whilst it is in the air, and watch it onto their foot. Body needs to be adaptable, only plant the non-kicking foot when the flight of the ball has been judged. Aim to get head and chest over the ball at the point of impact; this will help keep the strike low. Strike the middle of the football.

Best Practice Examples
Rebic [2018 WC] vs Argentina Mertens [2018 WC] vs Panama Pelle [Euro 2016] vs Belgium

Coach's Tip
Varying the angle of serves will allow the forward to practice both front volleys and side volleys.

Finishing Technique: Chip

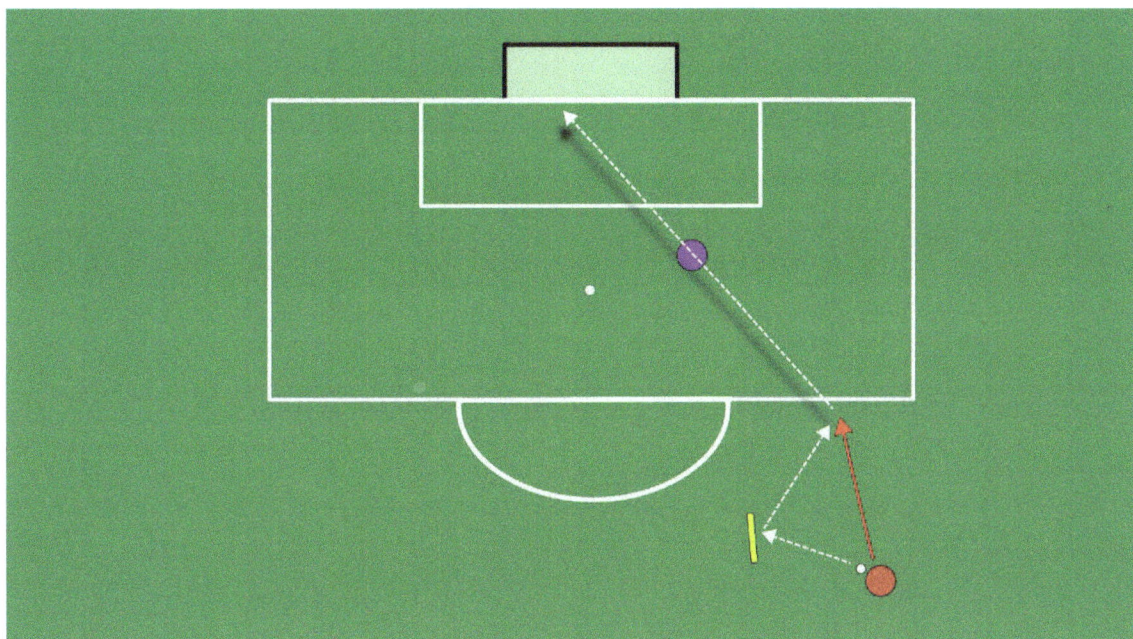

Practice	Key Technical Points
Coach positions himself as shown on the diagram. Forward passes the ball into the rebound board with the inside of the foot. As the ball comes off, at an angle, forward moves onto the ball and tries to chip the ball over the coach's head into the net. Technique can be first time or following a touch. 1 Repetition = 6 Balls.	The pass should allow for the forward to move onto the ball. Forward needs to get foot underneath the ball, leaning back slightly, and striking the ball with little to no follow through. The ball should cross the goal line without bouncing.

Best Practice Examples	Coach's Tip
Quagliarella [2010 WC] vs Slovakia Suker [Euro 96] vs Denmark Beckham [Euro 2004] Qualifier vs Macedonia	Encourage the technique of getting the ball up and down as opposed to favouring power.

Finishing Technique: Dinking the ball over a grounded goalkeeper

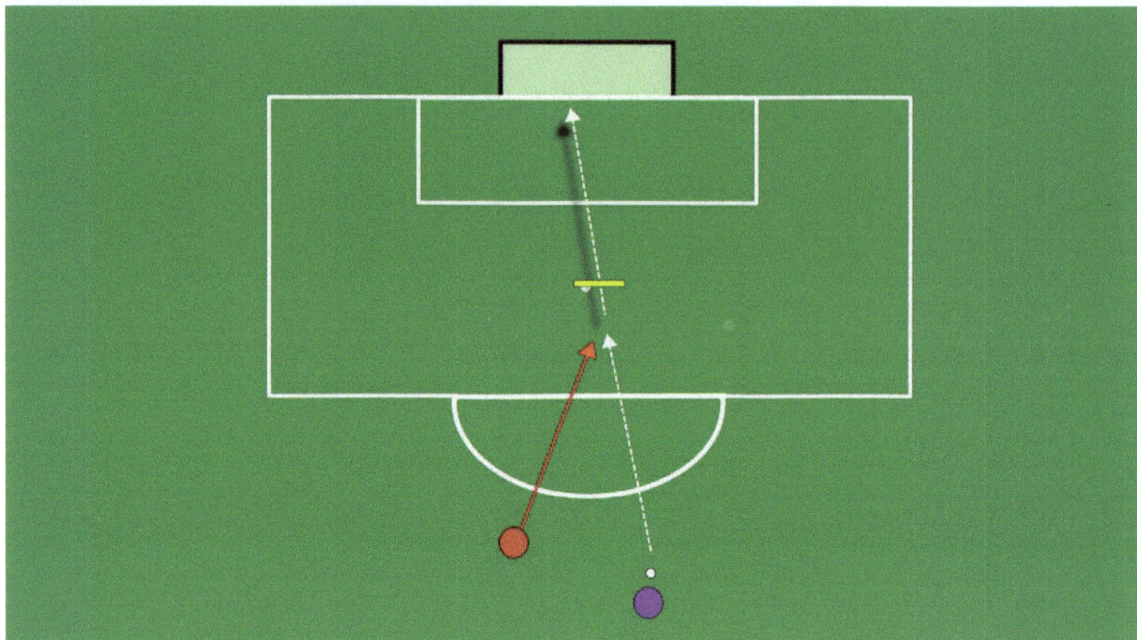

Practice

Coach takes a touch out of their feet and then passes the ball with the inside of the foot towards the rebound board.

On coach's touch, forward starts to run into the penalty box.

Forward looks to dink the ball over the rebound board and into the goal.

If the ball hits the rebound board, forward to score first time on the rebound.

1 Repetition = 6 Balls.

Key Technical Points

Forward's run to be done at speed.

Forward to get foot underneath the ball and flick it over the rebound board. Little to no follow through.

Take the shot first time if possible; if not, within two touches.

The ball should cross the line with maximum one bounce.

Stay alert after the initial shot, and ready for rebound if it comes back.

Best Practice Examples

Lukaku [2018 WC] vs Panama
Rodriguez [2014 WC] vs Japan
Griezmann [Euro 2016] vs Iceland

Coach's Tip

Getting underneath the ball is key here. Encourage forward to get body upright while dinking the ball.

Finishing Technique: Rounding the goalkeeper

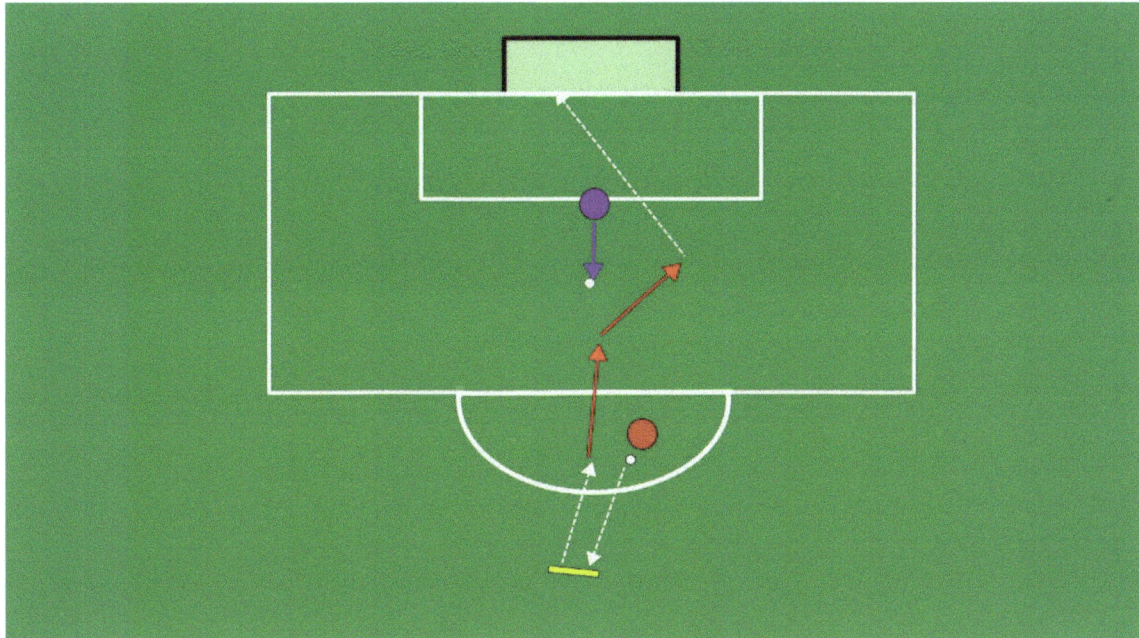

Practice

Pass the ball into the rebound board with the inside of the foot.

Turn and dribble at speed towards the goal. Coach (or GK) moves towards the forward either squatting or hunched over.

Forward goes around the coach (or GK) by accelerating quickly and then scoring.

Coach (or GK) looks to apply pressure to block the shot (not tackle).

1 Repetition = 6 Balls.

Key Technical Points

Drive towards the goal at speed, slowing down on approach to the GK.

Use of a feint to wrong-foot the GK.

Be unpredictable and able to go both ways

Accelerate past the GK, with a controlled touch.

Ensure accuracy of the finish.

Best Practice Examples

Pilar [Euro 2012] vs Russia
Robben [WC 2014] vs Spain
Ronaldo [2006 WC] vs Ghana

Coach's Tip

Challenge the forward to work at a match tempo when approaching the GK. This will help with applying the correct technique at speed.

Finishing Technique: Powerful Header

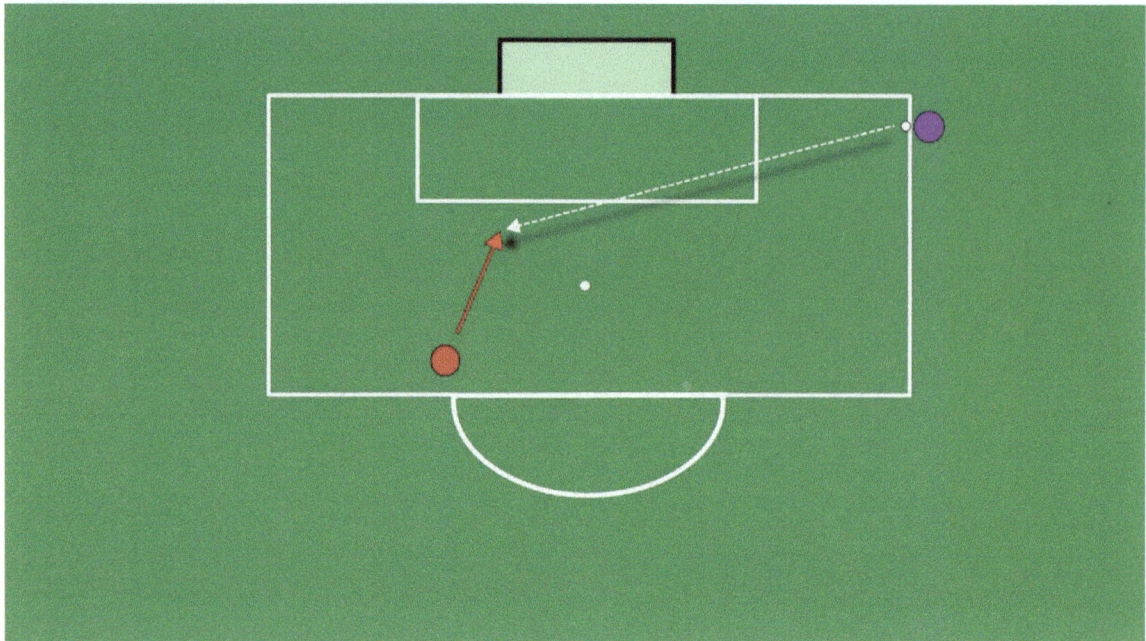

Practice

Coach bounces the ball and then throws the ball underarm into the area on the edge of the six-yard box. The throw should be looped up. Alternatively, the ball can be volleyed in by the coach.

The forward should start outside the line of the far post, and should look to attack the ball, heading it into the goal.

Practice serving the ball from both sides.

1 Repetition = 6 Balls.

Key Technical Points

The forward should be moving slowly, taking small steps until the ball is served.

Forward should judge the flight of the ball and make contact with the ball at the highest point possible, either jumping or standing.

Contact should ideally be with the forehead, using neck and shoulder muscles to generate power.

Watch the ball all the way.

Best Practice Examples

Carroll [Euro 2012] vs Sweden
Kane (2nd Goal) [WC 2018] vs Tunisia
Kokorin [2014 WC] vs Algeria

Coach's Tip

Encourage the header to be firm, downward, and the forward has their chest pointing towards the goal at the point of contact.

Finishing Technique: Flick Header

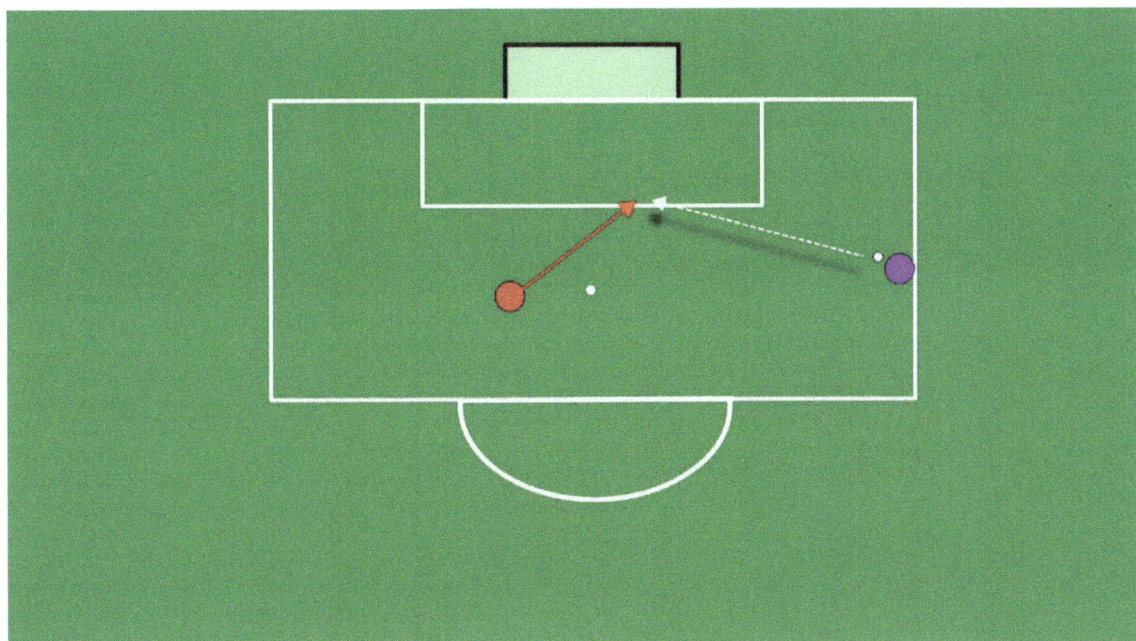

Practice

Coach bounces the ball and then throws the ball as a chest pass into the area on the edge of the six-yard box. The throw should be flat and powerful (just above head height). The ball can also be volleyed in by the coach.

The forward should start inside the line of the far post, and should look to attack the ball, heading it into the goal.

Practice serving from both sides.

1 Repetition = 6 Balls.

Key Technical Points

The forward should be moving slowly, taking small steps until the ball is served.

Forward needs to react quickly, and make contact with the ball as quickly as possible.

Contact should ideally be with the forehead, letting the ball hit the head and redirecting it towards the goal.

Watch the ball all the way.

Best Practice Examples

Morata [Euro 2016] vs Turkey
Bony [WC 2014] vs Japan
Dzagoev [Euro 2012] vs Poland

Coach's Tip

Encourage the player to use the speed on the ball and simply change the angle. Chest pointing towards the goal on the point of impact will help this.

Finishing Technique: Instinctive Finish

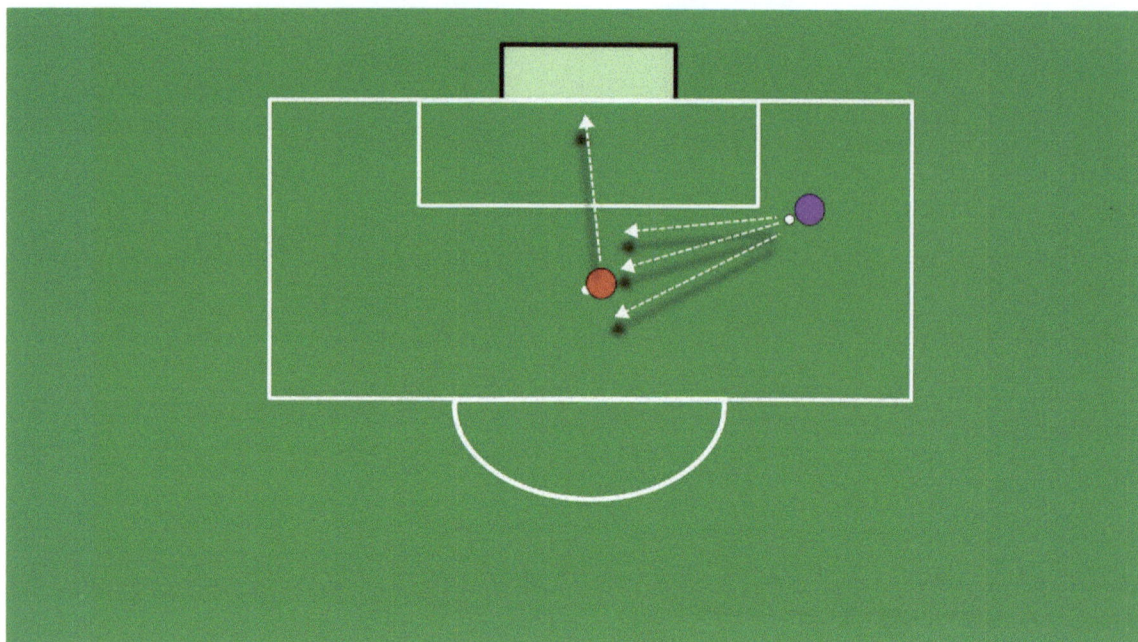

Practice

Coach bounces the ball and then throws the ball in towards the forward. The service should be of random height, speed, bounce, and angle.

The forward should start near the penalty spot and adapt to the flight of the ball, before finishing into the goal.

Forward to finish two-touch maximum.

Practice serving from both sides.

1 Repetition = 8 Balls.

Key Technical Points

The forward should be moving slowly, taking small steps until the ball is served.

Forward needs to react quickly, adapting to the flight and speed of the ball to make a clean contact towards goal.

Encourage a good contact with a solid surface.

Hit the ball downwards, as this will provide the best chance of hitting the target.

Best Practice Examples

Shaqiri [Euro 2016] vs Poland
Ronaldo [Euro 2016] vs Hungary
Villa [2014 WC] vs Australia

Coach's Tip

Allow creativity with the techniques required. Diving headers, overhead kicks, and back heels may be the most effective way of directing the ball towards goal.

Forward-Specific Practices

Over the next pages, you will find a number of practices to develop finishing. These sessions have been specifically designed in order to give coaches the opportunity to place forwards in match-realistic scenarios to develop the correct techniques in order to improve performances when it comes to matches.

With this in mind, there are number of points that should be remembered when planning and delivering these sessions with players.

Forward-specific sessions. These sessions are designed to put players in match-realistic scenarios, and whilst any player on the field may find themselves in this position at some point, the likelihood is that – more often than not – it will be a forward. These sessions are not designed to be completed by the whole team and, in particular, are not built for high numbers of players. Taking the correct number of players out of a 'whole team' session to work with one coach is the ideal situation for getting the best detail into the practice.

Correct equipment. If a coach wants their player to perform a particular action or task, and make it transferable to the game, then using the right equipment is imperative to this. The size of football, size of goal, and even the penalty area should be realistic to the player's age and development stage. The same is also true for practices that require a goalkeeper. Place a relevantly aged goalkeeper in the goals, as this will help develop a forward's understanding of what they will be coming up against.

Repetition. Each practice has a highlighted number of 'goes' before one repetition is complete. This ranges from a specific number (for example five balls) to a time limit (four minutes). During this time, the technical detail delivered by the coach may be in 'drive-by' form (the player is spoken to in-between serves) and it should not stop the practice. Following a completed repetition, there is a good opportunity for the coach and player(s) to discuss performance and highlight positives or areas for development.

Video analysis and feedback. Building on from the above point regarding repetition, video analysis is a powerful tool for developing an understanding of a player's individual technique. A static camera or tablet placed behind the forward can allow for feedback on performance and promote a healthy discussion between what the player feels they are doing and what they are actually executing. As before, limit feedback to after each repetition (not after each go) to allow the player to get into a flow for the practice.

Serving the ball. In the majority of the practices, the coach has been highlighted as a server, starting off the practice. The reasoning behind this is that the coach can control the speed of the session and dictate the tempo of how quickly the forward has to work and reset between goes. An alternative here is to use a player returning from injury, or a player from a different squad, in order to allow the coach to gain a different perspective of the practice. Either way, serves do not need to be perfect every time, and it is important that forward players adapt to the serve and finish the chance they are given.

The role of the defender. A number of the practices use defenders, in order to create a realistic challenge for the forward. As mentioned previously, space and time dictate much of what the forward can do within a situation, and placing pressure on them in practice is key to improving decision making. The role of the defender in these sessions should primarily be to invade the space of the forward, looking to block the forward's strike towards the goal. The defender should not be intercepting serves, flying into tackles, or barging forwards off the ball; this restricts the opportunity to practice, which is the main focus of these sessions. In directional games, where both teams are attacking and defending, regaining the ball with tackles and interceptions is expected.

Adapt and evolve. These practices act as a starting point for coaches to work with forward players and, through trial and error and experience, the coach will find the ones that work well for certain forwards. Others may need altering in order to get the best out of their particular players. This might include the type of service or the start position, for example, and coaches should play around with the setup of these practices to change the returns they may get. Change things around to keep the practices fresh for the players involved.

Session Diagrams

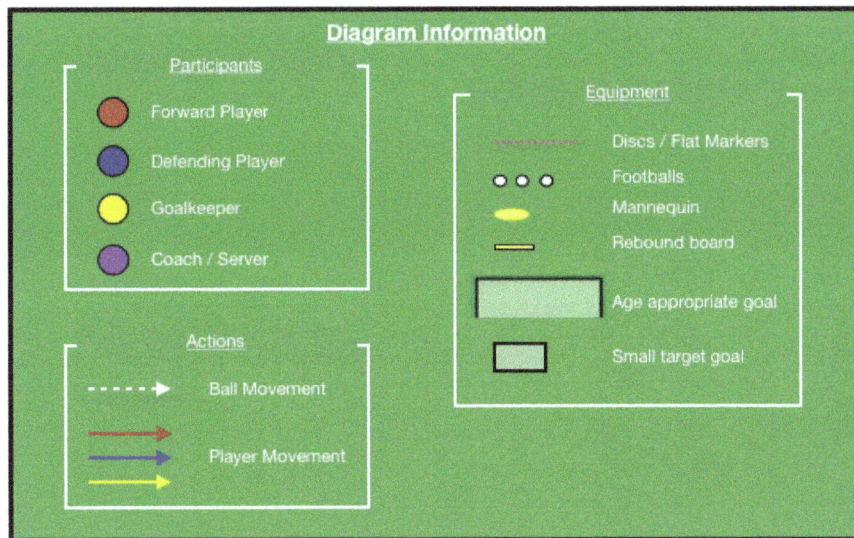

Diagram Information

Participants

- Forward Player
- Defending Player
- Goalkeeper
- Coach / Server

Actions

- Ball Movement
- Player Movement

Equipment

- Discs / Flat Markers
- Footballs
- Mannequin
- Rebound board
- Age appropriate goal
- Small target goal

1. Multiple One Touch Finishes

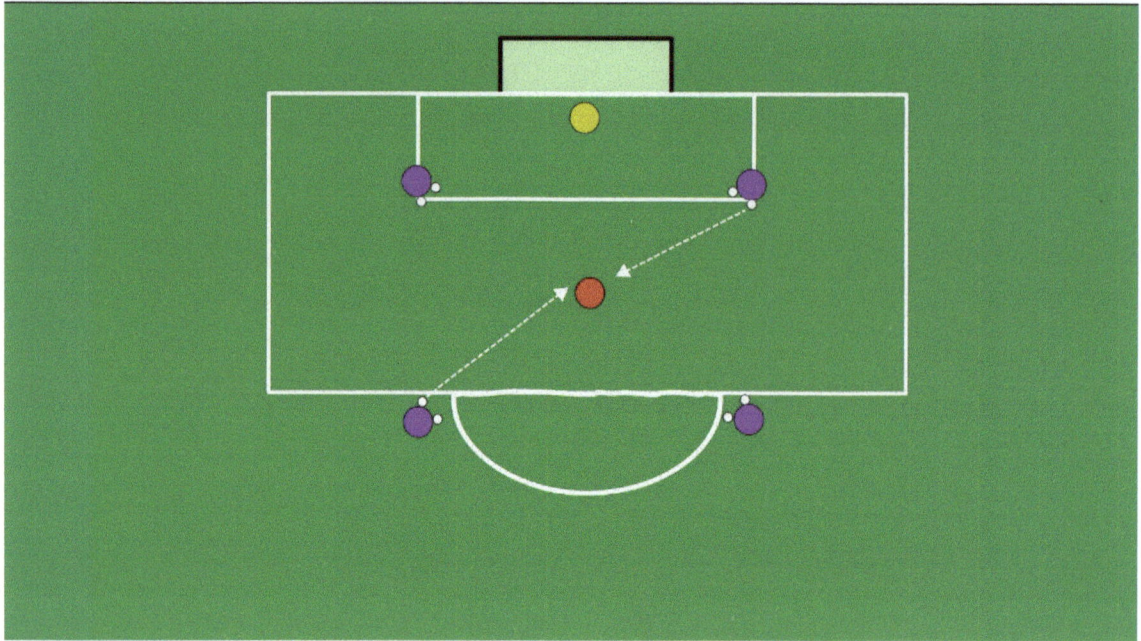

Practice

Four servers are positioned as shown, and given an order in which to serve the ball. They hold two balls, one under each arm.

The forward stands on the penalty spot as a starting point.

The first server places a ball on the floor and then serves in – quickly – to the forward, who tries to score first time. All other servers repeat.

On the second cycle, the first server bounces the ball and then throws the ball in to the forward, who again tries to finish first time. All other servers repeat.

1 Repetition = 8 Attempts at goal.

Key Technical Points

The trigger for the striker is the ball being put down / bouncing. As this happens, the forward should take a step away from the ball in order to give themselves more time to react.

As the ball is being served, the forward should work their body shape so they can see both the server and the goal.

Clean contact on the ball is needed to make sure it goes into the empty net.

Coach's Tip

Give the forward a three-second break between balls to allow them to reset. Ensure each finish is given the same attention and technique.

2. Heading Game

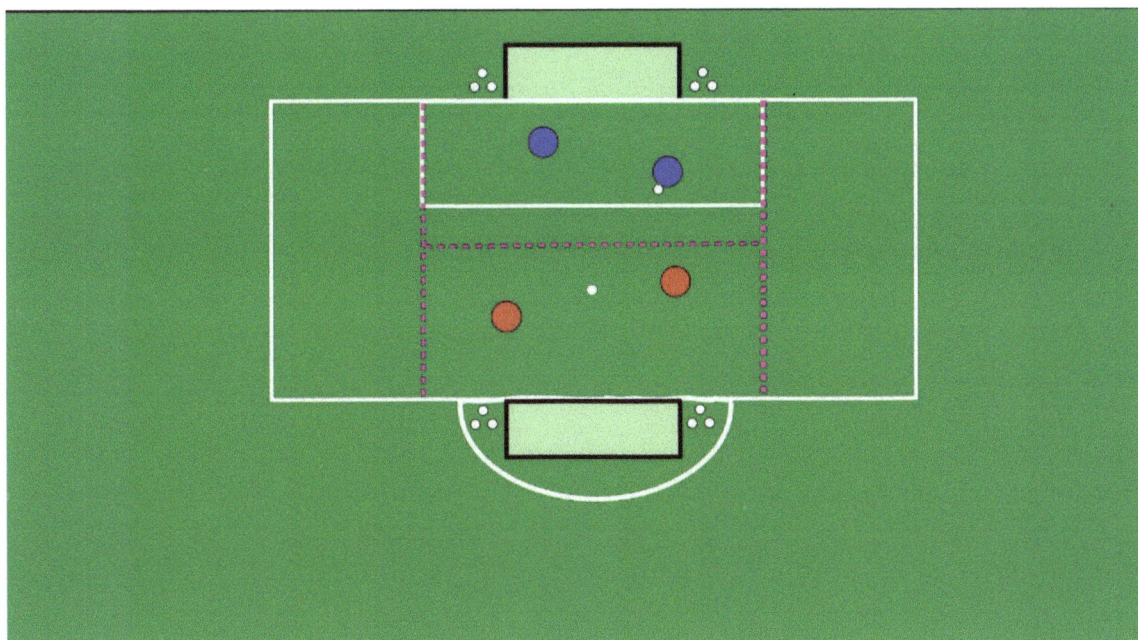

Practice

A 2 v 2 game working on heading towards goal.

The ball starts in the hands of one team. A player throws it to his teammate who attempts to head the ball into the goal past the opposing two players.

Players defending the goal cannot use their hands until the ball has bounced. They must block the attempt using feet / head / chest.

Once bounced, the defending team may pick the ball up and then do the same to try and score.

The attacking team can do multiple headers before heading towards goal.

1 Repetition = first team to 5 goals.

Key Technical Points

Body shape when heading the ball. Look to have the chest pointing towards the goal at the point of contact.

Keep eyes on the ball.

Be aware of the positioning of defenders and the type of throw. Power header or flick header.

If the ball is blocked, can the forward react quickly to head in a rebound?

Coach's Tip

Start with a central line which players may not cross to encourage good technique. As the game goes on, this line may be removed to develop opposed heading.

3. Rebound Finishing

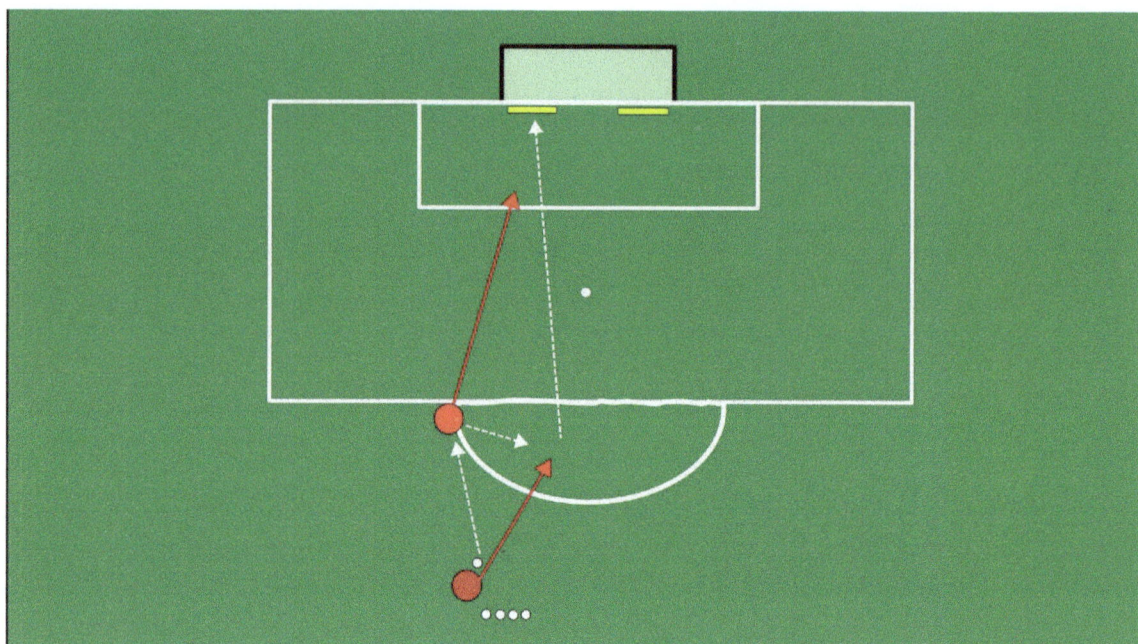

Practice

Forward 1 starts with the ball. It is passed into Forward 2 who sets the ball off at an angle.

Forward 1 aims to strike the ball, first time, to hit one of the two rebound boards, placed in the corners of the goal.

Forward 2 reacts to the shot, follows in the rebound, and finishes into the goal first time.

The practice should be run from both sides to encourage finishing first time from different angles

1 Repetition = Forward 1 and 2 have 5 goes each in both positions.

Key Technical Points

The shot from the edge of the area should be firm, with the laces. Keep the head over the ball whilst striking.

Forward 2 should be moving forwards before the ball is struck – getting in-between the posts.

React at speed as soon as the ball hits the rebound board.

The finish off the board should be controlled, keeping the head over the ball; it should be one touch.

Coach's Tip

Demand high standards on the rebound finish. You can turn the session into a competition between the two forwards to drive each other on.

4. Low Cross Finishing

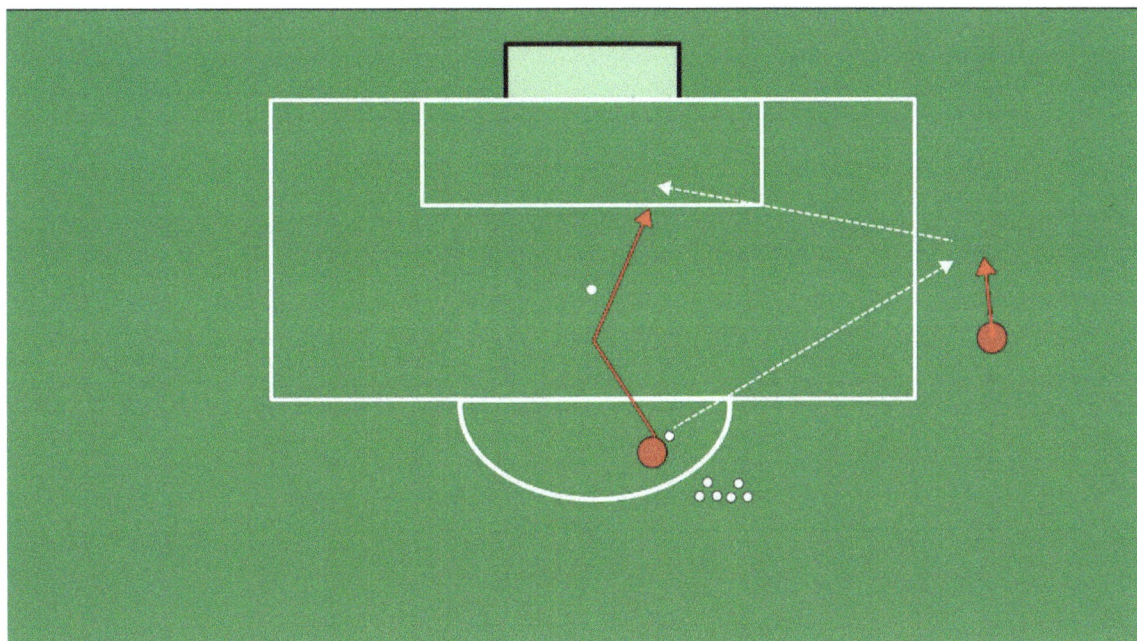

Forward 1 takes a touch out of feet and plays the ball wide, into the path of Forward 2

Forward 2 moves onto the pass and crosses the ball along the 6-yard box with the inside of the foot.

Forward 1 moves onto the cross and finishes first time.

Work from both sides to practice crossing and finishing with both feet.

1 Repetition = Forward 1 and 2 have 5 goes each in both positions.

Key Technical Points

Forward 1's pass should be in front of Forward 2, with a weight that allows the cross to be first time.

Double movement from Forward 1, firstly away from the ball then in towards the near post.

The cross from Forward 2 should be low and firm, in front of Forward 1.

Forward 1 to finish with front foot (right foot from the right-hand side), either inside of foot or laces.

Coach's Tip

The forward should keep their head still when making contact with the ball. The forward should make contact with the ball in-between the posts.

5. Back to Goal Finishing

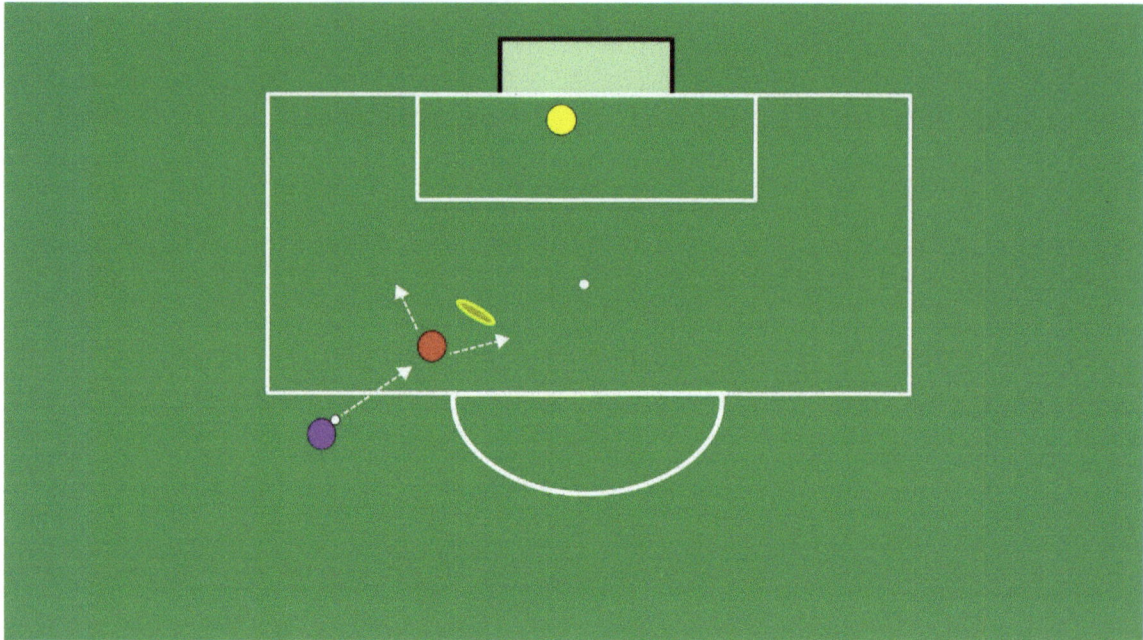

Practice

The forward starts by backing in towards the mannequin, before changing body shape to being sideways on to the coach.

Coach touches the ball, out of feet, and passes into the forward.

Forward takes one touch to turn before getting a shot away with a second touch past the GK.

Forward can turn either way (inside or outside).

Run the practice from both sides to develop turning and finishing from different angles.

1 Repetition = 6 Shots.

Key Technical Points

The trigger for the forward to change body shape is the coach's touch.

The forward's body shape should be sideways on, to create distance between the ball and mannequin.

Forward to turn with the front foot (the foot furthest away from the defender).

Practice using both the inside and outside of the foot to turn.

Finishing with laces or inside of the foot.

Coach's Tip

Encourage the forward to have their arm out to feel for mannequin. Encourage the spin and shot to be quick.

6. Angled Finishing

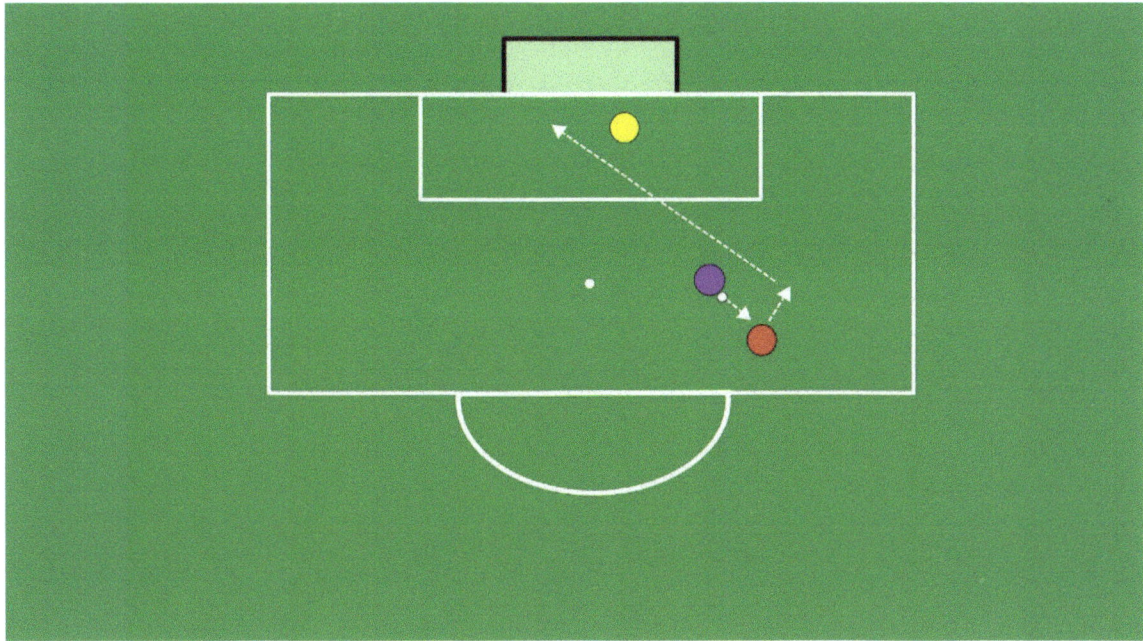

Practice

The forward starts opposite the coach, around 1m away.

Coach starts with their foot on the ball, takes it off, and quickly passes into the forward.

Forward takes one touch to the outside of the coach.

Forward strikes the ball across goal with their second touch.

Run practice from both sides to practice turning and finishing from different angles.

1 Repetition = 6 Shots.

Key Technical Points

The trigger for the forward is the coach taking their foot off the ball.

Depending on the pass, the first touch is with the outside of the right foot or the inside of the left (based on a shot from the right-hand side).

Forward to check up quickly after their touch to identify the GK's position.

Finishing with laces or inside of foot, ideally across goal.

Coach's Tip

The angle of the first touch should be diagonally forwards, cushioned, and not too wide – to allow for a stronger shooting opportunity.

7. Spin and Finish

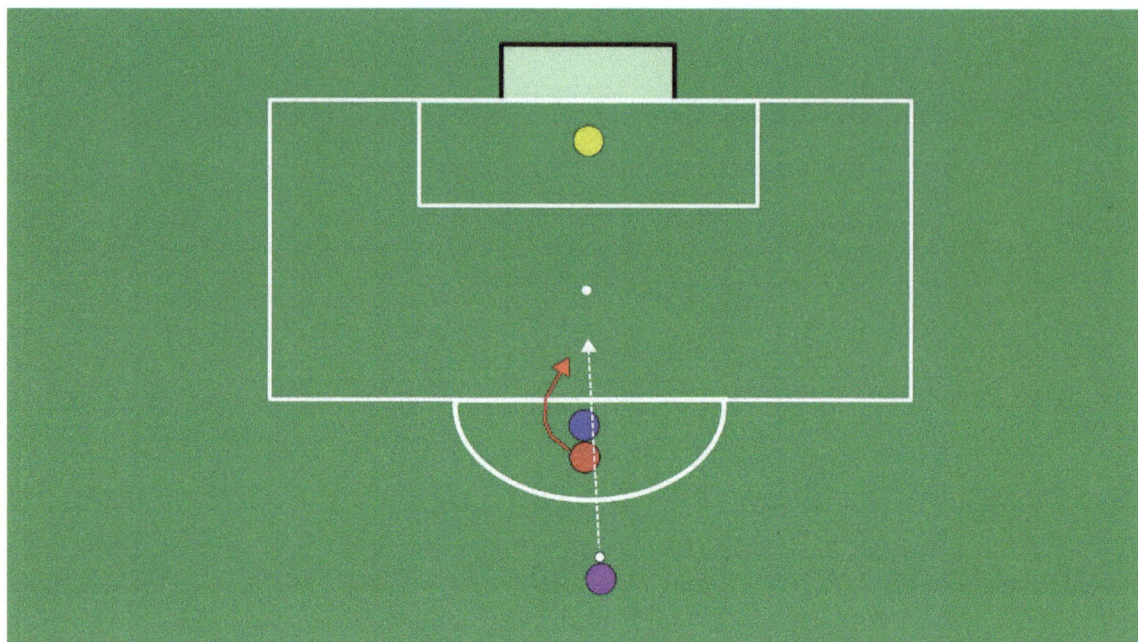

Practice

The forward starts opposite the coach, with the defender tight behind.

Coach bounces the ball and then throws the ball, underarm, over the forward and defender's heads.

Forward spins around and strikes the ball towards goal with one touch.

Defender starts off applying light pressure during the spin, but can add pressure to the finish in the second repetition.

1 Repetition = 5 Shots.

Key Technical Points

The trigger for the forward is the coach's throw.

Forward to use arm to feel for the defender. The spin should be tight to the defender and on the opposite side to where the forward feels the defender.

Forward should embrace physical contact, but not grab or push the defender.

Concentrate on getting the head over the ball during the finish. Placement is more important than power.

Coach's Tip

Reacting to the throw, and not going too early is key here. Encourage the forward to look up before the finish to identify the GK's position.

8. Crossing and Finishing

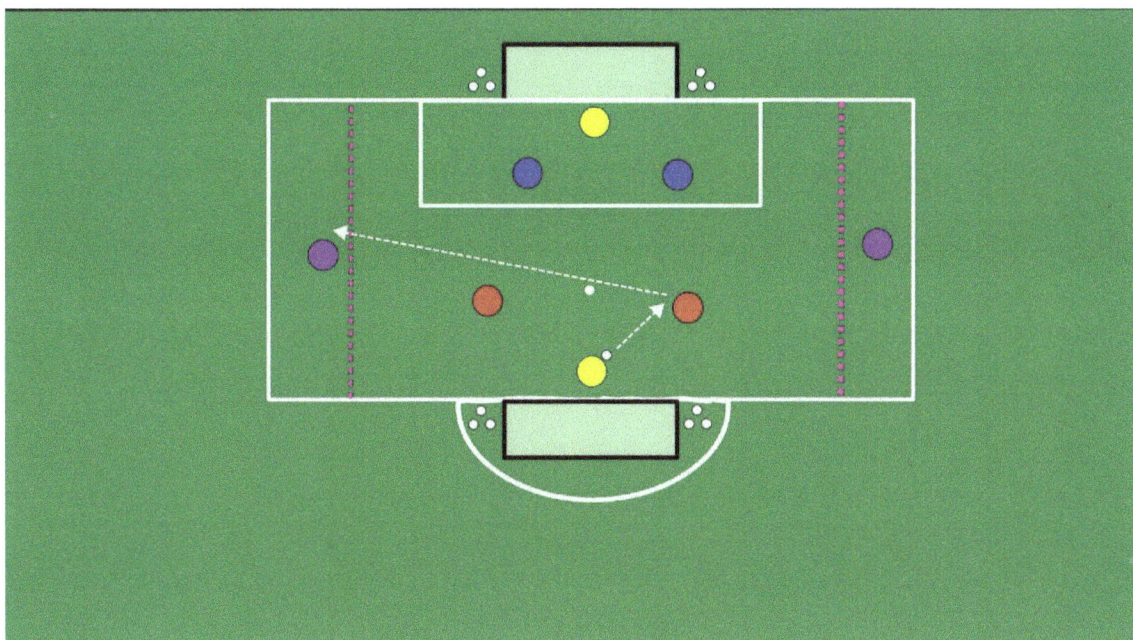

Practice

A 2 v 2 game with two servers (or coaches) on the outside of the area, and two GKs in the goals.

A directional game in which the red team must play out wide to either of the servers.

Each server has two touches to cross the ball into the area for the red team to try and score.

Finish must be within three touches of the cross or the ball must go back out to the server.

The game is directional, with blues attacking the opposite goal, and playing by the same rules.

1 Repetition = first team to 3 goals.

Key Technical Points

Combination play between two forwards in order to get the ball into the server.

The weight of pass into a server is important; either in front for a one touch cross, or to feet for a two touch.

Keep an eye on body shape when the server is crossing, the forward should be able to see the ball and the goal.

The forward should adapt their finishing technique to the flight of the cross, for example heading or volleying the ball. Clean contact on the ball and expect rebounds from the GK.

Coach's Tip

The two forwards should be aware of each other's positions, one makes a near post run, one goes to the far post. Communication as the ball is crossed is key.

9. Attacking the Ball to Finish

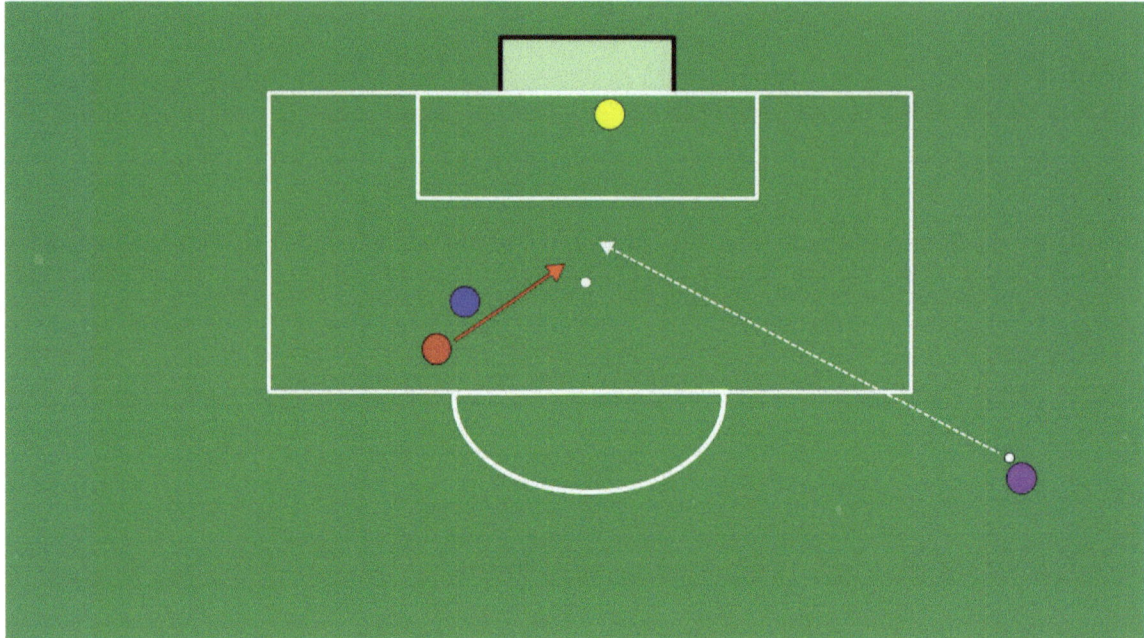

Practice

The coach takes a touch out of feet before serving the ball into the area, around the penalty spot. The serve can be along the floor or up to head height.

The forward makes a run across the defender and tries to finish with one touch.

Depending on the serve, the forward may need to take a second touch in order to finish.

The defender applies passive pressure, and is only allowed to block the forward's shot (cannot tackle or intercept the cross).

Work the practice from both sides.

1 Repetition = 5 shots.

Key Technical Points

The trigger for the forward's movement is the coach's first touch.

The forward can make a double movement, one away from the ball (short), before a run towards the ball.

Forward to make contact with the ball inside the line of the goal posts.

The forward's chest should point towards the goal on point of contact for the finish.

The forward should adapt their finishing technique to the flight of the cross, for example heading or volleying the ball.

Coach's Tip

The defender should start facing the forward with their back to goal. The forward's second movement needs to be sharp to create space for the finish.

10. Close Rebound Finishing

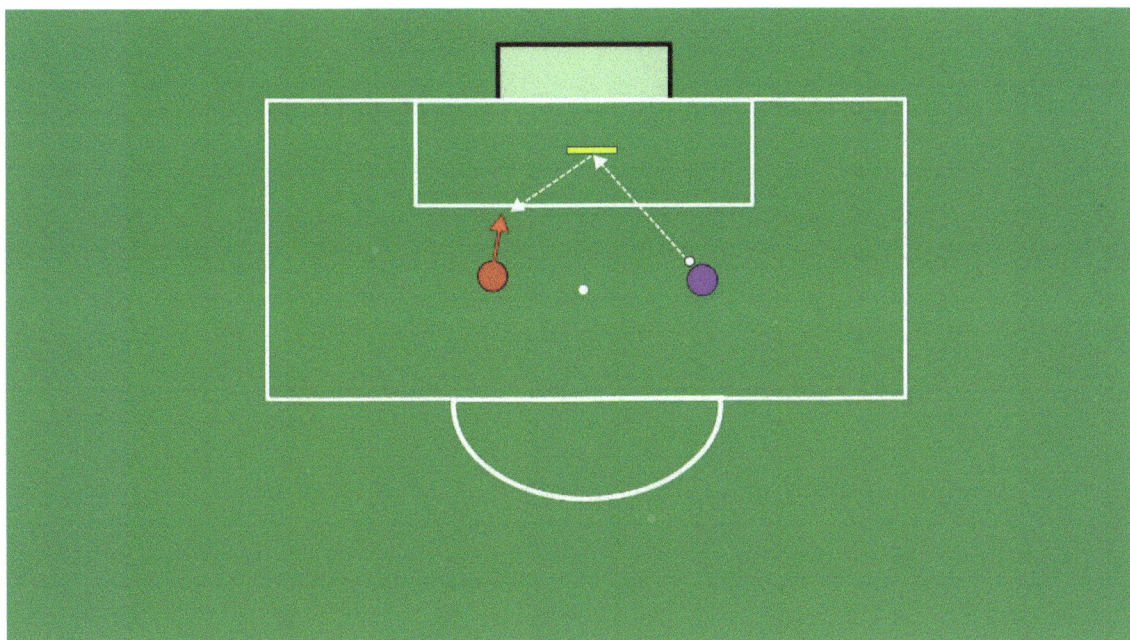

Practice

The coach plays the ball into the rebound board at an angle.

The ball will rebound back towards the forward who looks to finish first time.

If the ball comes in at an awkward angle or height, the forward may take a touch and then finish quickly with the second touch.

The coach should serve the ball from both sides to encourage the forward to work finishes with both feet.

1 Repetition = 6 shots from both sides (12 in total).

Key Technical Points

Short reaction time for the forward; encourage them to be light on their feet, ready to react.

The forward's body should be shaped to see the rebound board and the goal.

Finishing technique to be quick and efficient, being reactive to the bounce of the ball and its pace (laces / toe / inside / head / volley).

If a touch is taken, the finish should be clean and with accuracy into the corners.

Coach's Tip

Vary the speed and angle of the serve to encourage the forward to adapt their body shape and technique.

11. Across Goal Finish

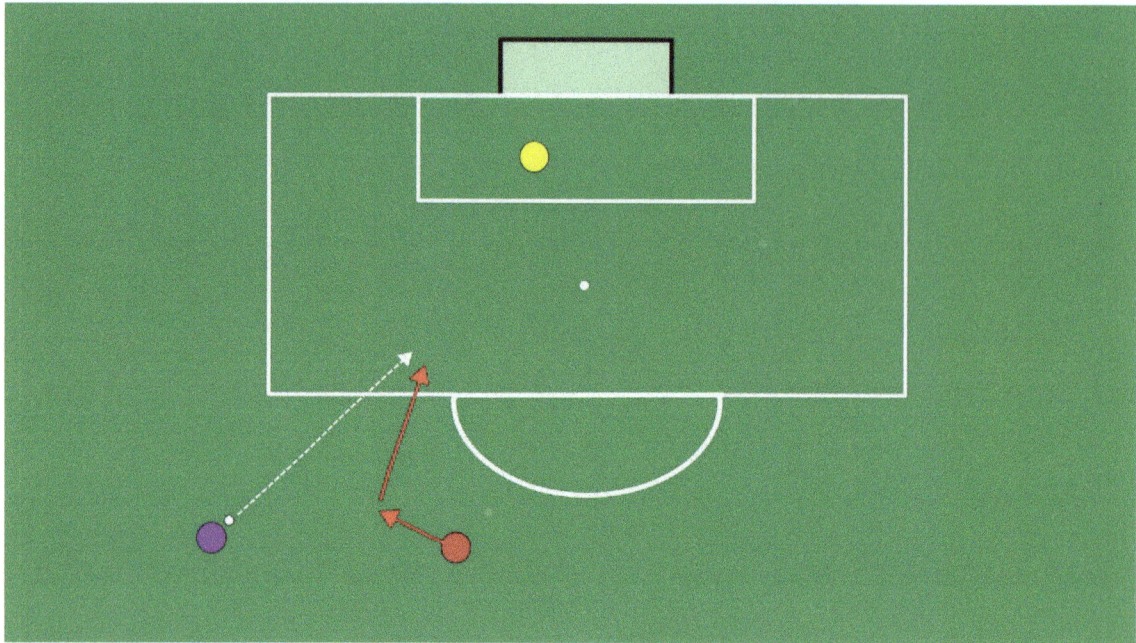

The coach takes a touch out of feet, followed by an angled through ball pass for the forward to run onto.

On the coach's touch, the forward moves towards the ball. Then, as the coach goes to play pass, the forward makes a run towards the goal.

The forward should finish past the GK, either one touch or two touch.

Work from both sides to give forwards the experience of different angles.

1 Repetition = 5 balls.

Key Technical Points

The trigger for the forward's movement is the coach's touch.

Speed and disguise is needed in the second movement to run onto the ball.

If finishing with the inside foot, open the body, point the chest at goal, and score in the corners.

If finishing with laces, strike through the ball, aiming for a corner.

A player should use their eyes (look one way) to trick the GK.

Coach's Tip

Forwards should accelerate onto the ball, then slow down when reaching the ball to focus on their finishing technique.

12. Wide Pass Finish

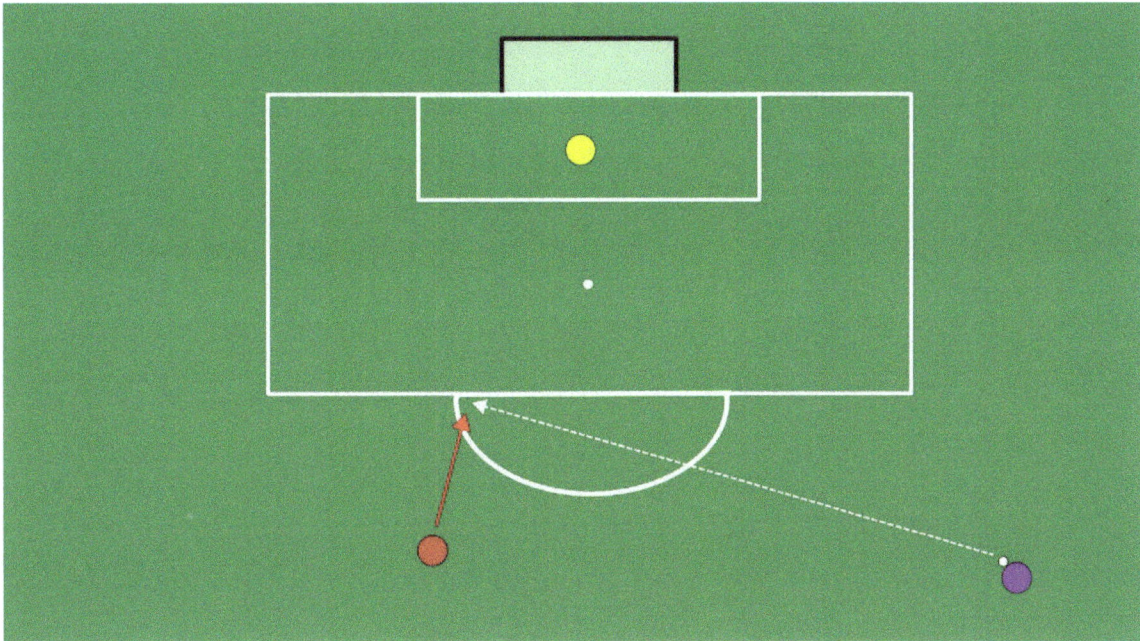

The coach takes a touch out of feet, then plays a diagonal pass into the edge of the area.

On the coach's touch, the forward starts moving towards goal, before reacting to the pass and meeting the ball.

The forward should attempt to finish inside the penalty area – either one touch if the pass allows it, or two touch if required.

Work from both sides to give the forward the experience of different angles.

1 Repetition = 5 balls.

Key Technical Points

The trigger for the forward's movement is the coach's touch.

The timing of movement is key; judge the pass and meet the ball in its path… don't get ahead of the ball.

If a first touch is required, it should be cushioned, into the path, and allow for the next touch to be a finish.

Look up to see the GK's position.

Each finish should be controlled and on target.

Coach's Tip

The player's body shape – when looking to receive the pass – should be open so they can see the ball and the goal.

13. 2 v 2 Finishing Game

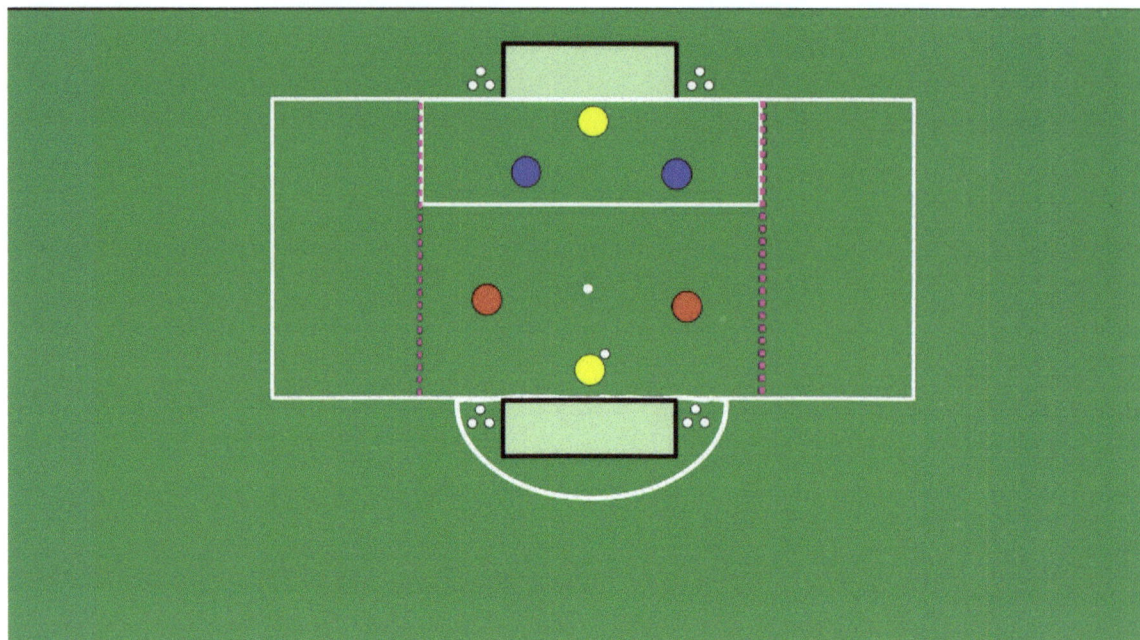

Practice

A 2 v 2 game working on finishing in the area.

The ball starts with the red GK, who rolls the ball into one of the two red players.

The red team look to combine and finishing in the opposing goal.

If the blue GK gets the ball, or the blues regain the ball, they look to shoot in the opposing direction.

GKs are allowed to roll, throw or pass the ball out with feet.

No corner kicks or throw ins. If a ball is saved by a GK, or the defending team puts the ball behind, play starts with the opposing GK.

1 Repetition = 3 minute game.

Key Technical Points

Get the right body shape when receiving the ball. The forward should be able to see the goal if possible.

Quick and clever combination play, give and goes, one touch play, and individual skill to create space for a shot.

Look to shoot quickly when the opportunity arises. Technique is relevant to the space and scenario.

The second forward should expect rebounds.

Coach's Tip

This session is high tempo, so encourage a quick flow of footballs when the ball goes out of play. Encourage the forwards to shoot, and the defenders to block shots.

14. Quick Finishing

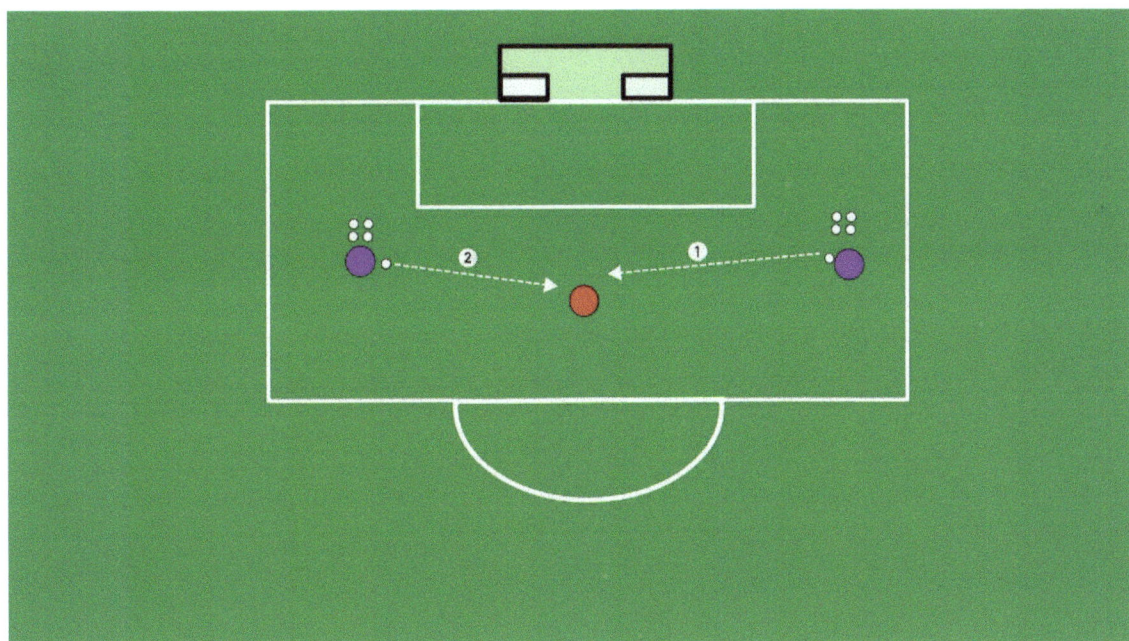

Practice

Two coaches position themselves with five balls each. Coach 1 passes a ball across, into the feet of the forward.

The forward finishes either one touch, or two, into either of the small goals, positioned in the corner of the big goal.

Coach 2 allows two seconds for the forward to reset their position, then passes a ball into the forward who repeats the finishing task into the other goal.

The sequence is repeated until the forward has finished all 10 balls.

1 Repetition = 10 balls.

Key Technical Points

This is a reaction practice. The forward must be ready for the pass with no trigger. They need to be light on their feet.

The correct body shape will enable the forward to see the coach who is passing the ball and the goal.

If finishing first time, finish with the front foot (the foot nearest the coach, the left foot from the left side).

If taking a touch, receive the ball on the back foot. All finishes should be controlled and accurate.

Coach's Tip

Whether laces, or with the inside of the foot, ensure the forward gets their head over ball and their chest aims towards goal at the point of shooting.

15. Combination Finishing

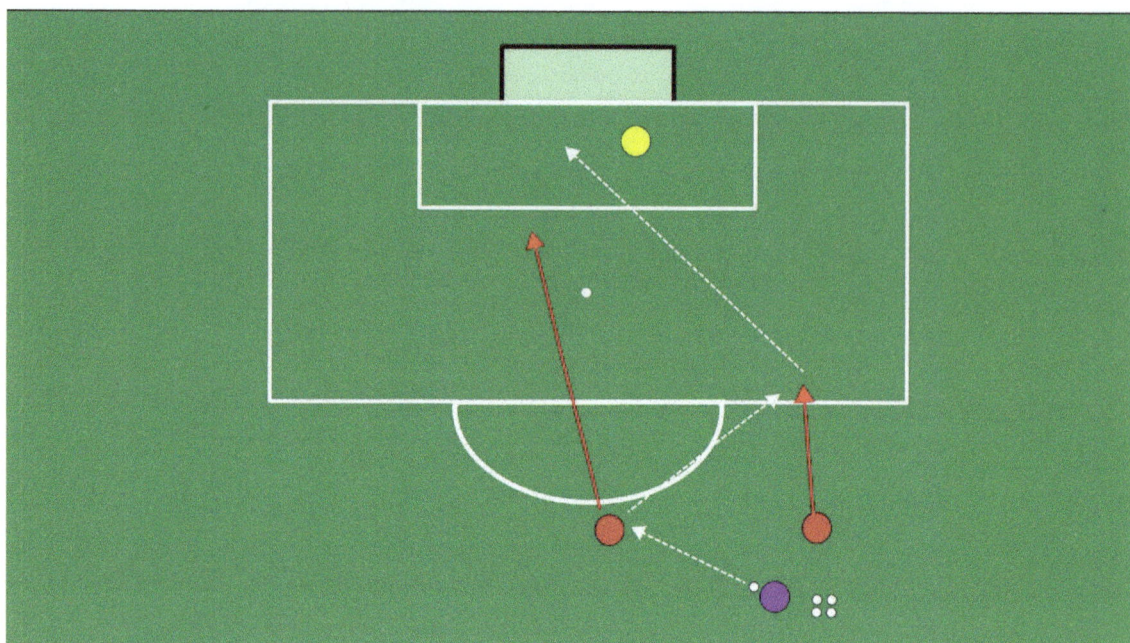

Practice

The coach takes a touch of feet and passes the ball into Forward 1.

Forward 1 passes the ball with one touch in front of Forward 2.

Forward 2 runs onto the ball. Depending on the angle, Forward 2 chooses whether to shoot at goal, or cross the ball. This should be done one touch.

Forward 1 moves towards the 6-yard box, either to finish the cross or collect the rebound off the GK.

Work from both sides.

1 Repetition = Each forward has 5 finishes.

Key Technical Points

Forward 1's pass should be on the front foot, 'around the corner', in front of Forward 2.

Forward 2 should hold their run until the pass is made, but have their weight forwards, ready to run.

Forward 2 should strike across goal either with laces or the inside of the foot. Aim for the far post.

If crossing, ensure it is with pace and in front of Forward 1.

Coach's Tip

Forward 1 should expect the cross from Forward 2, and the run into the box (towards the back post) must be sharp with a sprint if needed. Forward 1's finish must be one touch, whether from a cross or rebound.

16. Through-Ball Finishing

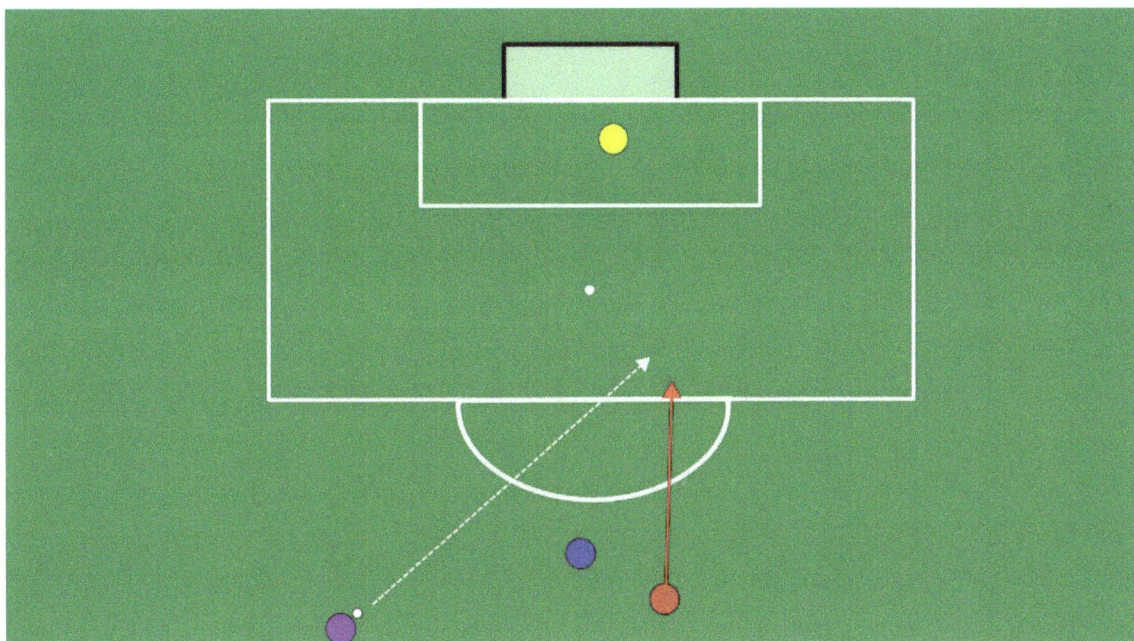

The coach takes a touch out of feet and passes the ball into space behind the defender (the defender should start by looking at the ball).

The forward runs onto the through ball and looks to finish with one touch or two touches if needed.

The defender looks to recover back towards goal and aims to block the shot (not tackle the forward).

The GK must stay in the 6-yard box for the first repetition, but can come out for the second repetition if desired.

Work from both sides to give the forward the experience of different angles.

1 Repetition = 6 finishes.

Key Technical Points

The trigger for the forward's run is when the coach's head goes down to start the pass.

The correct body shape should allow the forward to see the ball and goal as they are running onto the pass.

The forward should adapt their pace and angle of run to meet the pass.

The use of arms to hold off the defender should be encouraged.

Finishes should be controlled and towards the goal's corners, either with laces or the inside of the foot.

Coach's Tip

As the GK comes into play, dinking, toe poking, and rounding the GK are potential finishing options. Encourage a quick finish to take the defender out of the game.

17. Across Defender Finishing

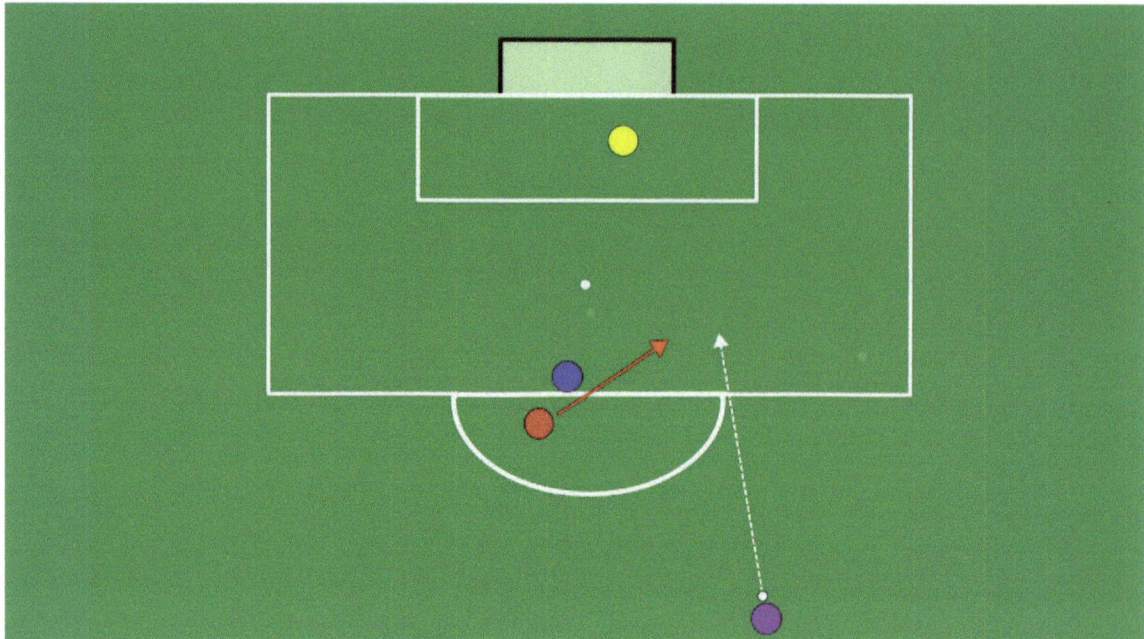

Practice

The coach takes a touch out of feet and passes the ball into space in front of the forward, on a slight diagonal.

The forward runs in front of the defender to meet the pass.

The forward finishes, ideally with one touch or two touches. If this is not possible, find a way of creating space to shoot.

The defender may only block the shot of the forward, not tackle or intercept the pass.

Work from both sides to give the forward the experience of different angles.

1 Repetition = 5 finishes.

Key Technical Points

The forward should start from a standstill / moving slowly. Acceleration is the key to creating separation from the defender.

The trigger for the forward's run is when the coach's head goes down to pass.

Run in front of the defender.

Adapt the angle of the run to meet the pass.

Every finish should be controlled and towards the corners, either with laces or the inside of the foot.

Coach's Tip

The defender should start quite static, looking at the ball to help the forward with movement. Encourage a quick finish to take the defender out of the game. A feint may be needed if the defender gets close.

18. Run from Behind Finishing

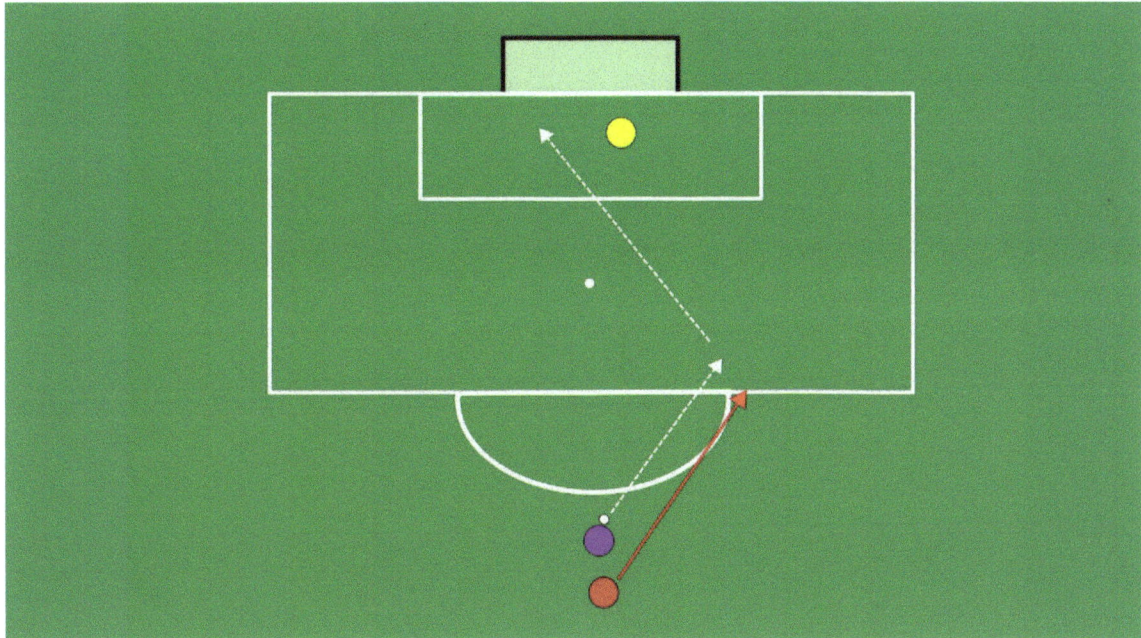

Practice

The coach takes a touch out of feet either to the left or right. They then pass the ball diagonally the opposite way into the space in front of the forward.

The forward runs onto the through ball and looks to finish with one touch.

Coach can alternate which side they choose to take their touch.

The GK must stay in the 6-yard box for the first repetition, but can come out for the second repetition if needed.

1 Repetition = 6 finishes.

Key Technical Points

The trigger for the forward's run is when the coach takes their first touch. Run on the opposite side to where the touch is taken.

Run to the ball at full speed then slow down a few steps before to gain balance.

Look up before finishing to identify the GK's positioning and the type of finish required.

Be aware of rebounds off the GK.

Coach's Tip

As the GK comes into play, dinking, toe poking, and rounding the GK are potential finishing options; multiple touches may be required.

19. Aerial Finishing

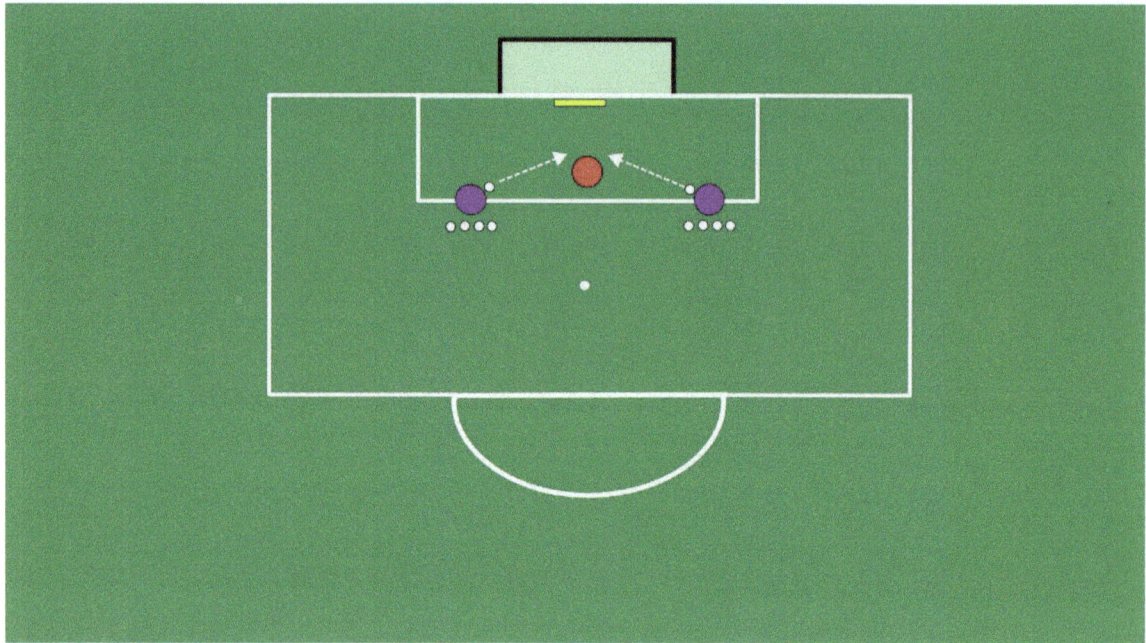

Practice

Two coaches position themselves with five balls each. Coach 1 throws the ball across to the forward, either with a chest pass or underarm throw.

The forward should finish with one touch anywhere in the goal, avoiding the rebound board. The ball should not bounce.

Coach 2 allows two seconds for the forward to their reset position, then passes a ball into the forward who repeats the task.

The sequence is then repeated until the forward has finished all 10 balls.

1 Repetition = 10 balls.

Key Technical Points

This is a reaction practice. The forward must be ready for the pass with no trigger. They need to be light on their feet.

The correct body shape to see the coach who is passing the ball and the goal.

The finish will be dependent on the throw. If heading, aim down and towards the goal's corners. If volleying, the head and chest should be over the ball.

If the ball hits the rebound board, react for a one touch finish.

Coach's Tip

The forward should watch the ball onto the foot or head, and concentrate on each finish individually. Encourage a high tempo and control in finishing.

20. One Touch Finish

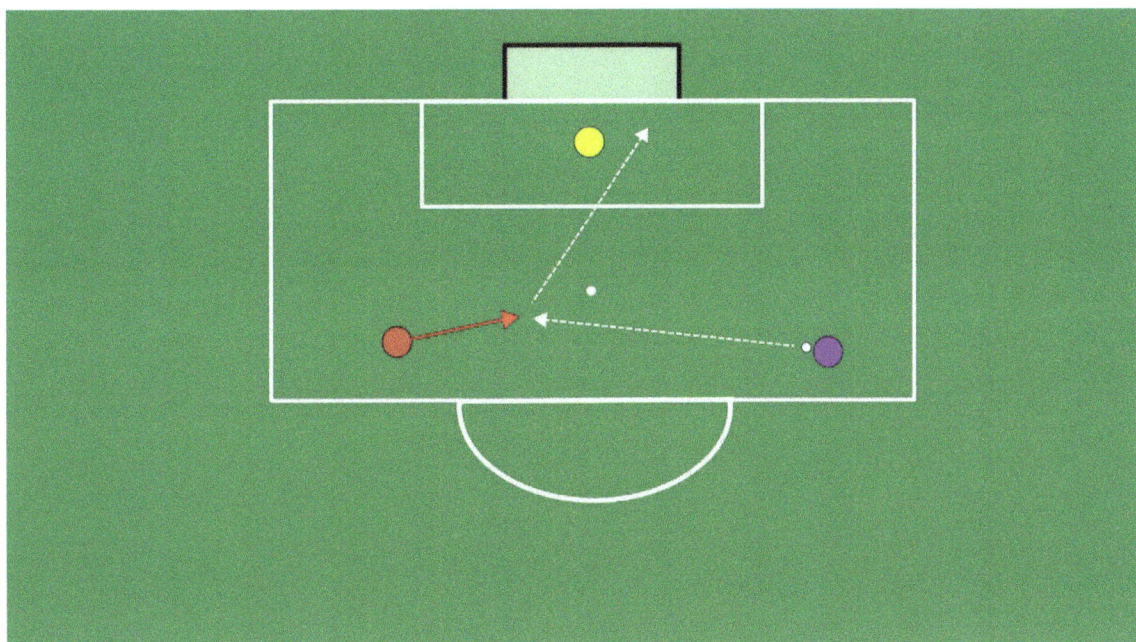

Practice

The coach takes a touch out of feet, then plays a diagonal pass across to around the penalty spot.

On the coach's touch, the forward starts moving forward, before reacting to the pass and meeting the ball.

The forward should look to finish first time, meeting the ball on the run.

Work from both sides to give the forward the experience of different angles.

1 Repetition = 5 balls.

Key Technical Points

The trigger for the forward's movement is when the coach passes the ball.

Timing of movement; judge the pass and meet the ball in path. A slow pass means a quicker run. A faster pass means a slower run.

Head over the ball when striking to finish. Finish with the front foot (right foot from the right side).

The finish should be controlled, using either laces or the inside of the foot.

Coach's Tip

Encourage the finish to go back across goal (a right-side pass means finishing in the right-side of the goal). The forward should be balanced when striking the ball.

21. One on One Finishing

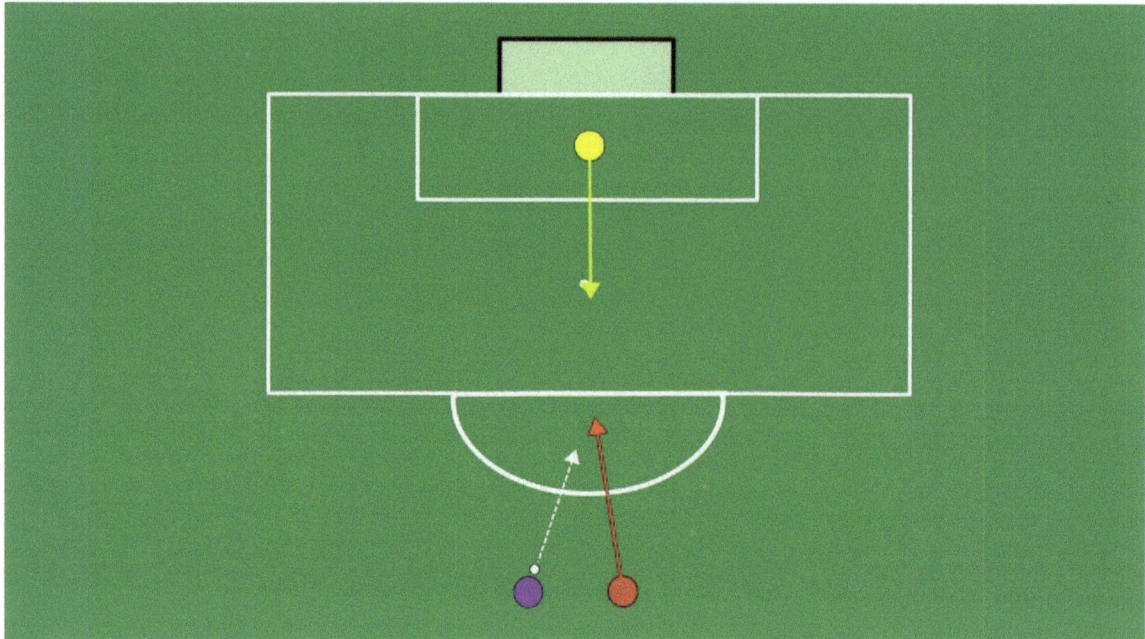

Practice

The coach passes the ball into the space in front of the forward. The forward should start level with the coach.

The forward runs onto the through ball. At the same time, the GK makes a decision whether to stay on their line or close down the angle.

The forward makes a decision on how to finish, based on position, angle, and the GK's location.

The forward should make runs from different angles, to help develop decisions based on different positions.

1 Repetition = 5 finishes.

Key Technical Points

The trigger for the forward's run is when the coach's head goes down to pass.

The forward runs at full speed, slowing down around 1m away from the football.

Head up to check the position of the GK to make the decision on the type of finish required.

Use disguise when finishing; drop shoulder or use eyes to confuse the GK.

Each finish should be controlled and clean.

Coach's Tip

Depending on the GK's position, dinking, toe poking and rounding the GK are potential finishing options. Encourage a quick decision to make things more difficult for the GK.

22. One-Two Finishing

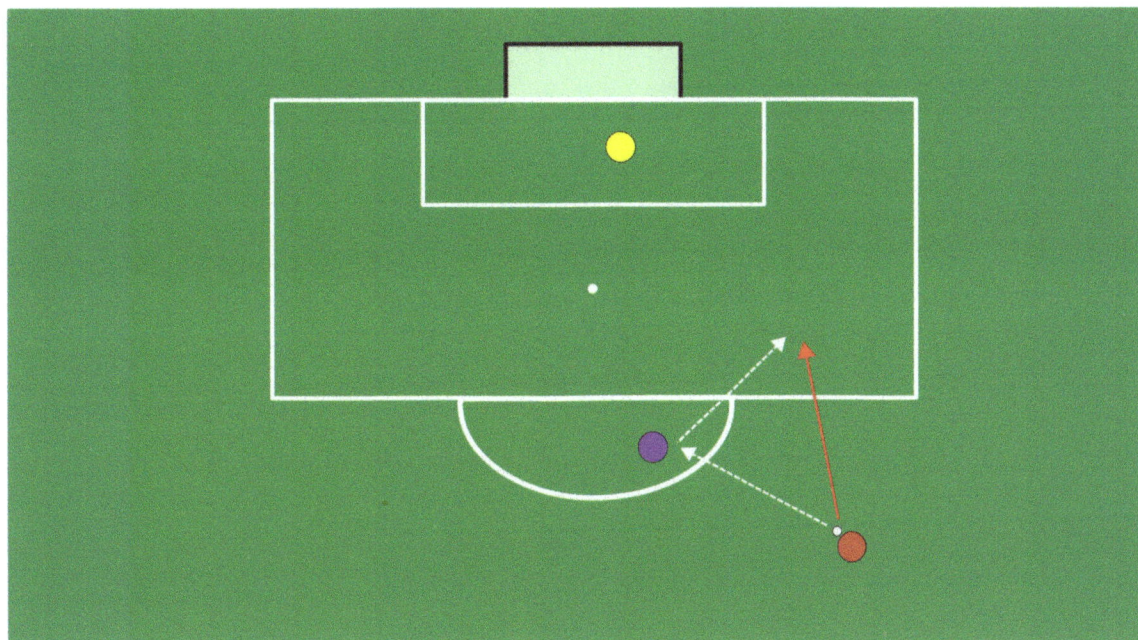

Practice

The forward takes a touch out of feet and plays the ball into the feet of the coach.

The coach passes the ball into the space in front of the forward, ideally using one touch.

Forward 1 moves onto the ball and finishes first time.

Work from both sides to practice crossing and finishing with both feet.

1 Repetition = 6 finishes.

Key Technical Points

The forward should play the pass with the outside of the foot (left foot from the right-hand side).

The forward's run should be controlled, until the coach plays a return pass, before accelerating away.

The forward should finish across the goal, aiming for the far post, either with laces or the inside of the foot.

The player should run towards the goal after their shot, to be in position for a rebound.

Coach's Tip

Vary the angle and pace of the return pass to the forward. Encourage the forward to adapt their pace and finish to the return pass.

23. Tight Marking Finishing

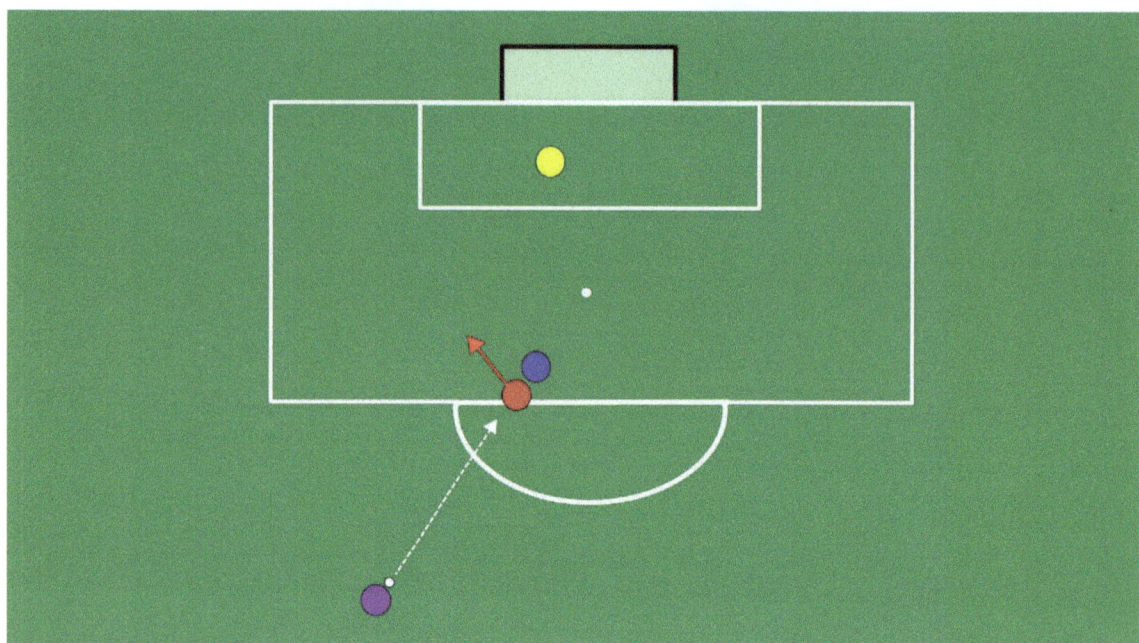

Practice

The forward starts by backing in towards the defender, before changing their body shape and being sideways on to the coach.

The coach touches the ball out of feet and passes into the forward.

The forward receives the ball under pressure, either turning with their first touch, or protecting the ball to turn on the second touch.

The forward gets their shot away having turned.

The defender starts passively, looking to the block shot. The second repetition may allow for the defender to apply more physical pressure.

Run the practice from both sides to practice turning and finishing from different angles.

1 Repetition = 6 Shots.

Key Technical Points

The trigger for the forward to change body shape is the coach's touch.

The forward's body shape needs to be sideways on, to create distance between the ball and defender.

The forward receives the turn with the front foot (furthest away from the defender). They use their body to protect the ball.

The forward should turn both ways, using sole, and inside / outside, of the foot. A quick shot after any turn is needed.

Coach's Tip

Encourage the defender to apply pressure, blocking any shot as opposed to tackling the forward. Encourage the forward to feel the defender's positioning and turn the opposite way.

24. One against One Finishing

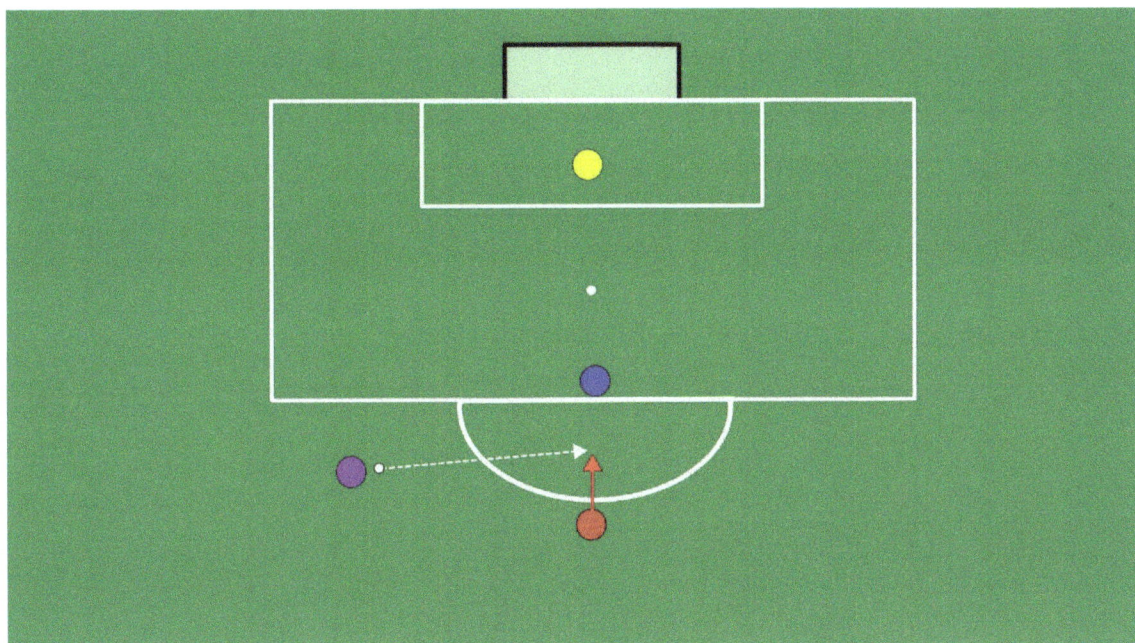

The forward starts on the edge of the D; the defender starts just inside the penalty area.

The coach passes the ball into the D, and the forward moves into the D to receive the ball.

The defender must stay in their area.

The forward can shoot from either inside or outside the area. The defender may tackle inside the area, but can only block when the forward is outside.

If the forward enters the area, the ball is not allowed out again.

The defender scores by returning the ball to the coach.

1 Repetition = 6 passes in by coach, 3 from either side.

Key Technical Points

The forward's first touch creates an angle for an early shot, out of feet and to one side.

Use the defender's body to hide the ball from the GK.

A quick shot with the inside of the foot, laces, or a toe poke, to catch GK out is desirable.

If entering the area, the forward should use feints and disguise to create angles for a shot.

Stay in the game if the shot is blocked.

Coach's Tip

The forward should vary their finishing techniques and style. Encourage a drop of the shoulder to create space for a shot.

25. Rebound Finishing

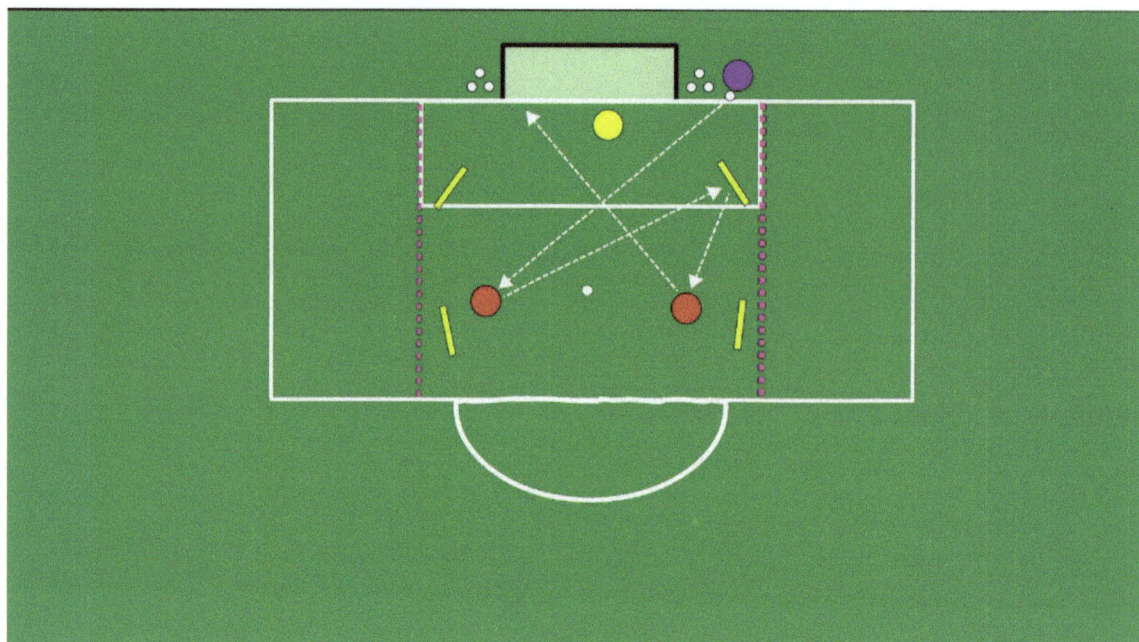

The coach starts with the ball by the side of the goal. Forward 1 calls for the ball and the coach passes the ball into feet.

Forward 1 has two touches to pass the ball against a rebound board.

Forward 2 reacts to the pass off the rebound board and finishes with one touch.

The forwards should alternate roles in order for both to get a chance at finishing.

1 Repetition = 10 passes in by coach, 5 from each side. Forwards to decide who sets and who finishes.

Key Technical Points

Forward 1 makes an angle before calling for the ball in order to see the coach and the rebound board.

Forward 2 takes a position up off Forward 1, able to see the ball and the goal.

The passing technique from Forward 1 should be firm, either with the inside of the foot or laces.

Forward 2 should be light on their feet and ready to react with a controlled finish.

Coach's Tip

The forwards should be moving around in-between turns. Encourage good technique on the finish, aiming for the goal's corners and striking the ball firmly.

26. Quick Combination Finishing

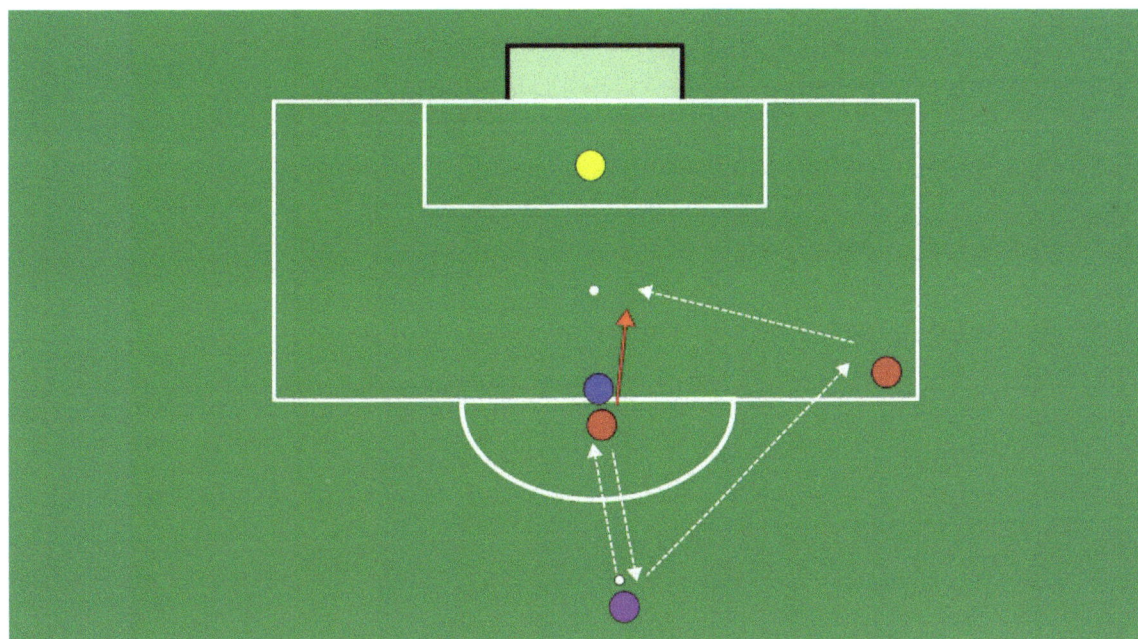

Practice

The coach takes a touch out of feet and passes the ball into Forward 1.

Forward 1 passes the ball back to the coach, first touch if possible.

The coach plays the ball wide to Forward 2.

Forward 2 crosses the ball into the area, in front of Forward 1.

Forward 1 runs in to finish first time.

Both forward players can be 'offside' if the movement isn't timed correctly.

Forwards 1 and 2 switch roles. Work the practice from both sides to encourage finishing with both feet.

1 Repetition = both forwards have 5 turns in each role.

Key Technical Points

The pass from Forward 1 should be first time, and soft enough for the coach to pass first time.

Forward 2 receives whilst stood still, and looks to play first time into the space in front of Forward 1.

Forward 1 should run in front of the defender and finish with their front foot (right foot from right side).

The player should keep their head still when finishing. They should deliver a controlled finish and make sure they hit the goal.

Coach's Tip

The defender should apply some pressure on the edge of the area, and then block any shot, not tackle or intercept. Forward 1 should show sharp movement to create distance from the defender.

27. Running-Through Finishing

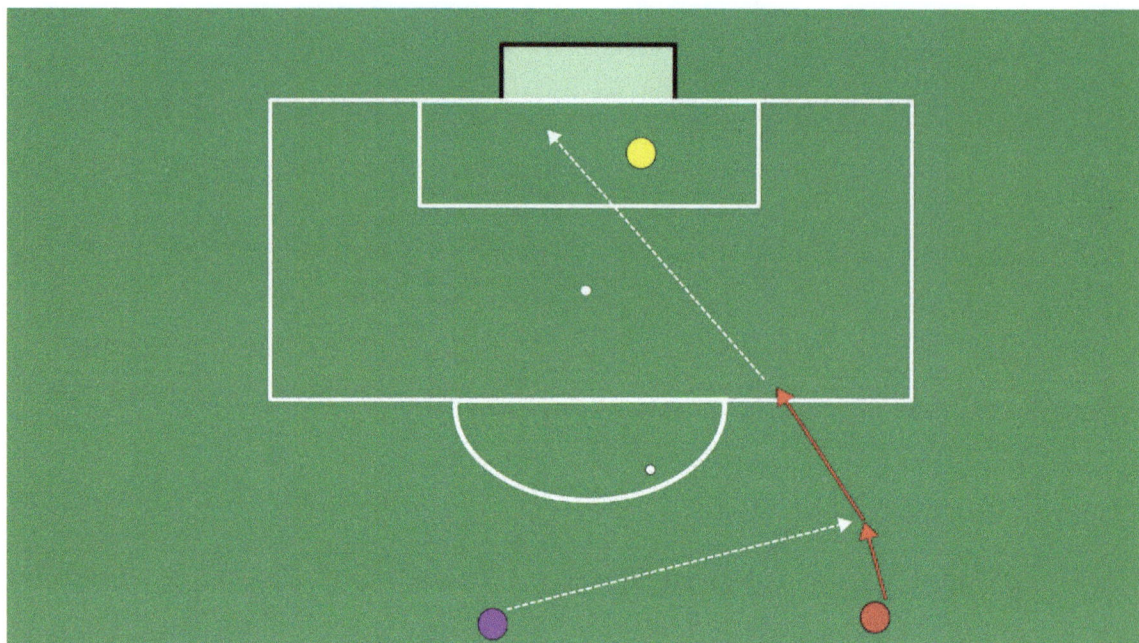

The coach takes a touch out of feet and passes the ball into space in front of the forward.

The forward starts their run on the coach's touch and then receives the ball.

The forward runs with the ball into the penalty area.

The forward should finish across goal, past the GK.

Work from both sides to give the forward the experience of different angles.

1 Repetition = 6 finishes.

Key Technical Points

The trigger for the forward's run is the coach's first touch.

The player's body shape should allow them to see the ball and goal as they run onto the ball.

First touch with inside of foot, allowing the forward to run onto the ball into space.

Head up to see the GK's position.

The finish should be controlled, head over the ball, with laces.

Coach's Tip

Encourage the forward to slow down when getting into the area to gain balance and control. Make sure the forward doesn't take their touch too wide.

28. High Cross Finishing

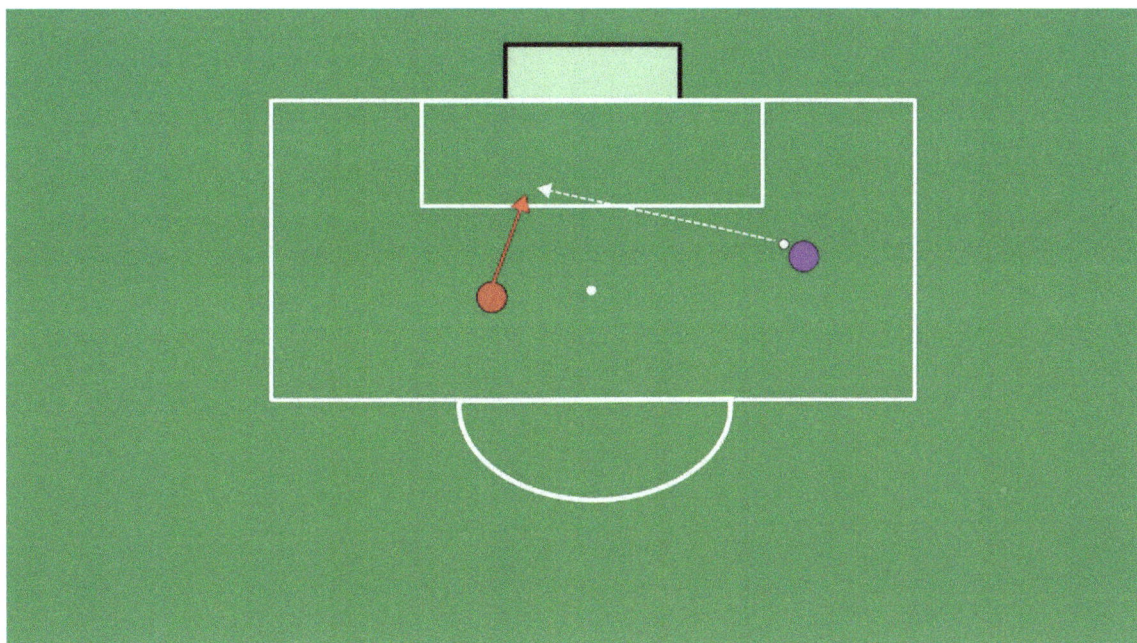

Practice

The coach bounces the ball and then serves it into the 6-yard box. The serve can be an underarm throw, overarm throw, or volley from hands.

The forward judges the flight of the ball and makes contact, finishing first time into the goal.

The forward must attempt to finish before the ball bounces.

Work from both sides to practice finishing from both angles.

1 Repetition = 6 finishes.

Key Technical Points

The trigger for the forward to become ready is as the ball bounces. Move slowly until ball is in the air and then judge where to meet it.

Adopt a body shape to see both the ball and goal, if possible. Eyes on the ball.

A clean contact, either with head or foot, is paramount. Technique is relevant to the height and pace of the ball.

Head over the ball at point of contact if possible, to keep the finish down.

Coach's Tip

Vary the type of serve to challenge the forward's finishing technique. Make sure the forward starts moving as the ball is bounced; little steps outside the line of the goal.

29. Edge of Area Finishing

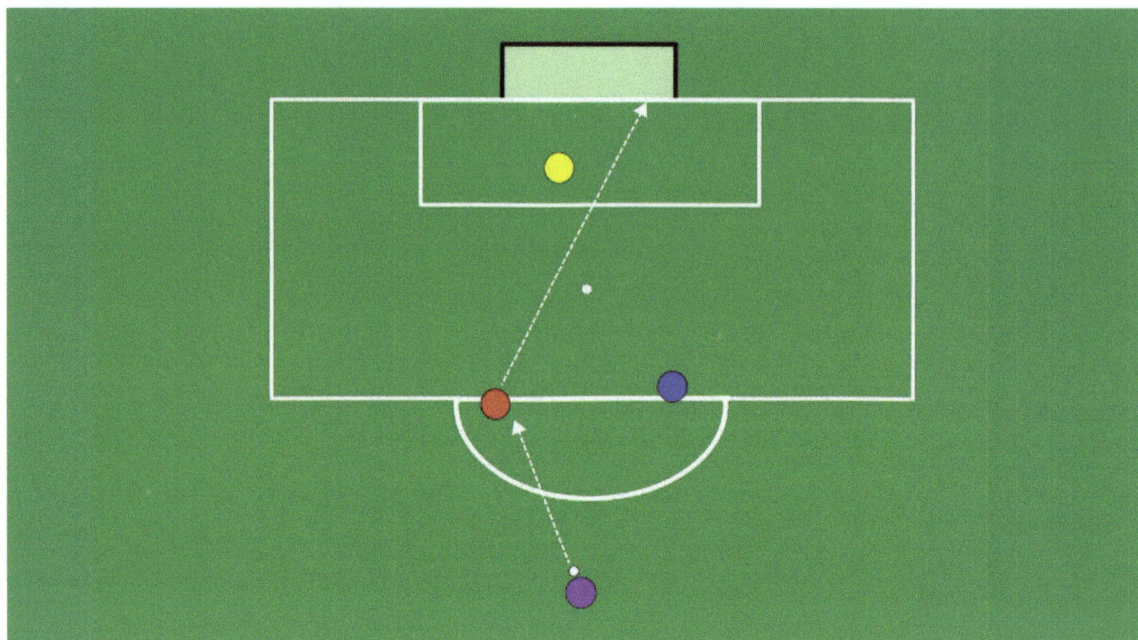

Practice

The coach passes the ball into the feet of the forward, who is positioned on the edge of the penalty area.

The forward decides whether to take a touch and then finish, or let the ball run across their body to finish in the area.

As soon as the coach passes the ball, the defender can recover, and look to block the shot of the forward.

The GK is in play, and can decide to come off their line.

Work from both sides to give the forward the experience of different angles.

1 Repetition = 5 finishes.

Key Technical Points

The forward to start from a standstill / moving slowly.

The trigger for the forward's decision is the weight of the pass from the coach. Too soft or hard means having a touch; a controlled weight of pass may allow for the ball to run across the body.

If taking a touch, the player should receive sideways on, and take the first touch with the back foot.

The finish should be quick, either with laces or the inside of the foot from the edge of the area.

Coach's Tip

Vary the passing to give the forward a chance to receive the ball or let it run across. If in the area, any decision on the type of finish should be based on the positioning of the GK, with dinking, rounding the GK, or toe poking all being options.

30. Second Phase Finishing

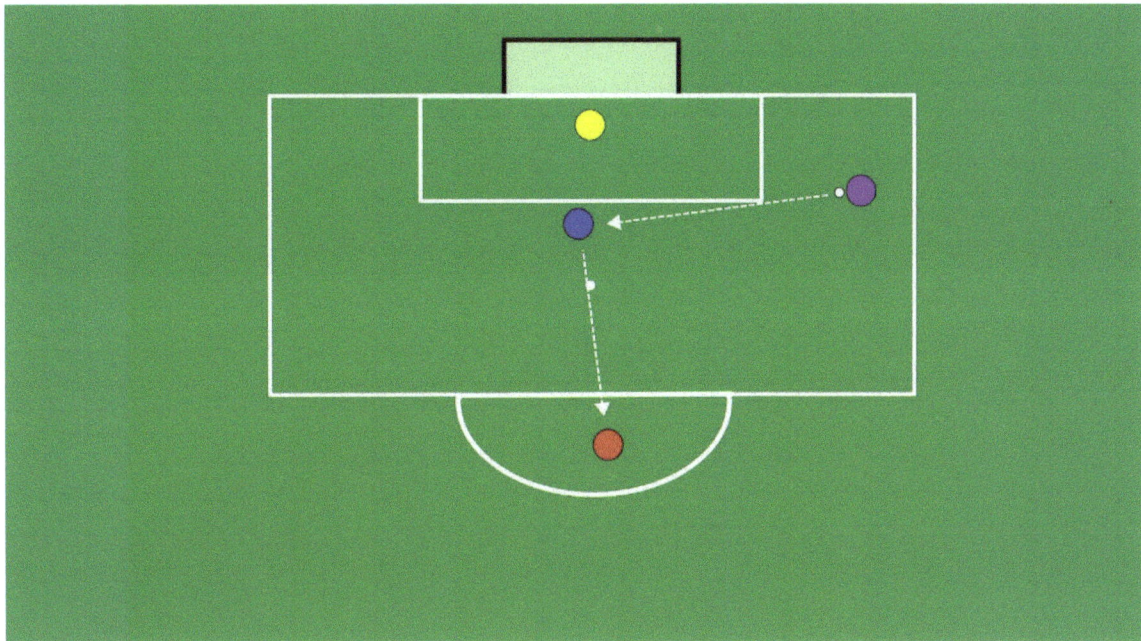

Practice

The coach serves the ball into the defender, who clears the ball into the forward. This can be done either on the floor or with a header.

The forward decides whether to finish with one touch, or take a touch and finish with the second touch.

As the ball is cleared, the defender can apply pressure to the forward. The defender looks to block the shot, not tackle or intercept.

The Coach should serve from both sides to provide different angles for the forward.

1 Repetition = 5 finishes.

Key Technical Points

The forward should be light on their feet on the edge of the area, and judge where the defender's clearance is going to land.

The forward's decision whether to finish first time should be based on the flight and speed of the ball.

If controlling the ball, cushion it to one side to allow for the second touch to be a shot. Use feints or disguise on the first touch to create space.

The forward's head should be over the ball to keep it down.

Coach's Tip

The type of finish is relative to the ball; a volley if in the air, or laces / inside of the foot / toe poke / chip if the ball is on the floor. The player should look up after any first touch to make their decision.

69

Session Templates

Over the next few pages, you will find a number of blank templates designed to be filled in with your own forward-specific coaching sessions.

The idea here is to keep all your practices together in one place, creating a personal library for delivering these types of sessions.

They follow a similar template to the practices in this book, with an additional box designed for you to fill in your notes after you have delivered your first session, in order to inform your own practice or how you deliver the session in the future.

Session Name:

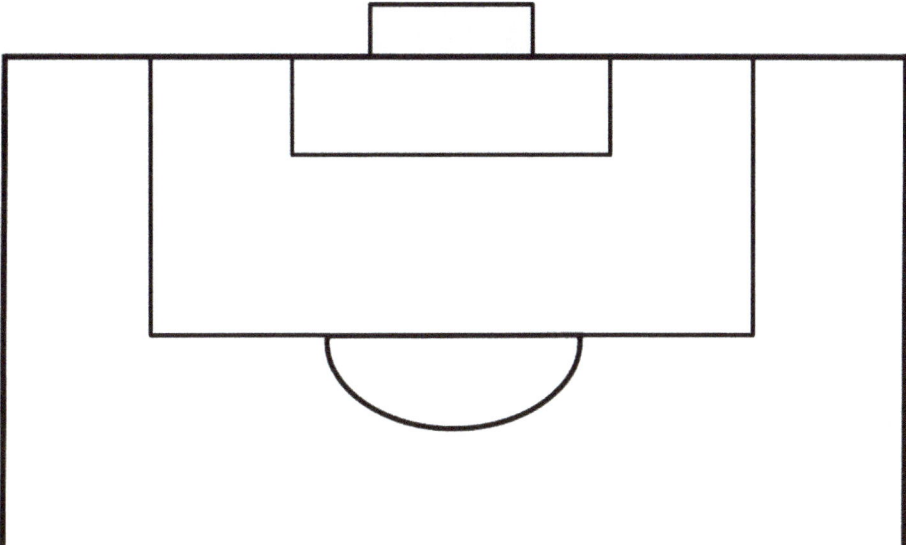

Practice	Key Technical Points

Notes for Next Time
(What went well, what you'd change)

Session Name:

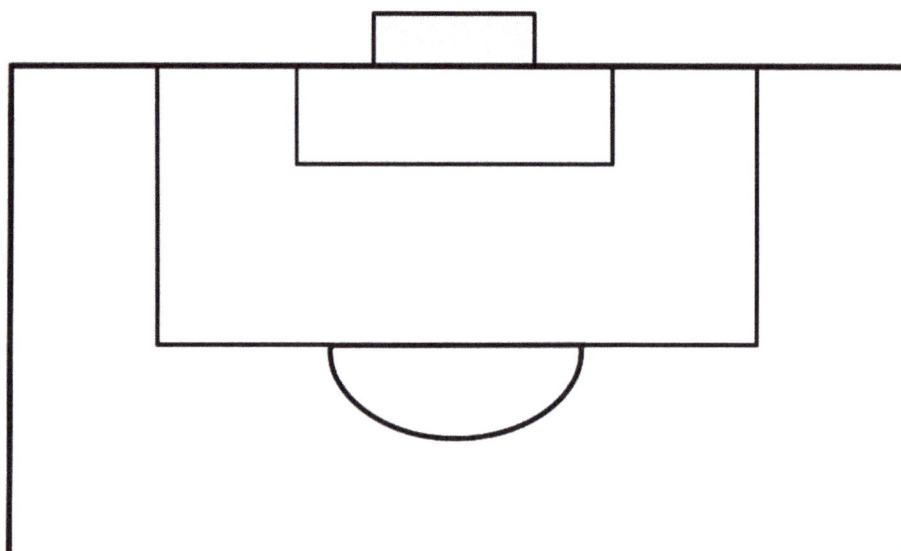

Practice

Key Technical Points

Notes for Next Time
(What went well, what you'd change)

Session Name:

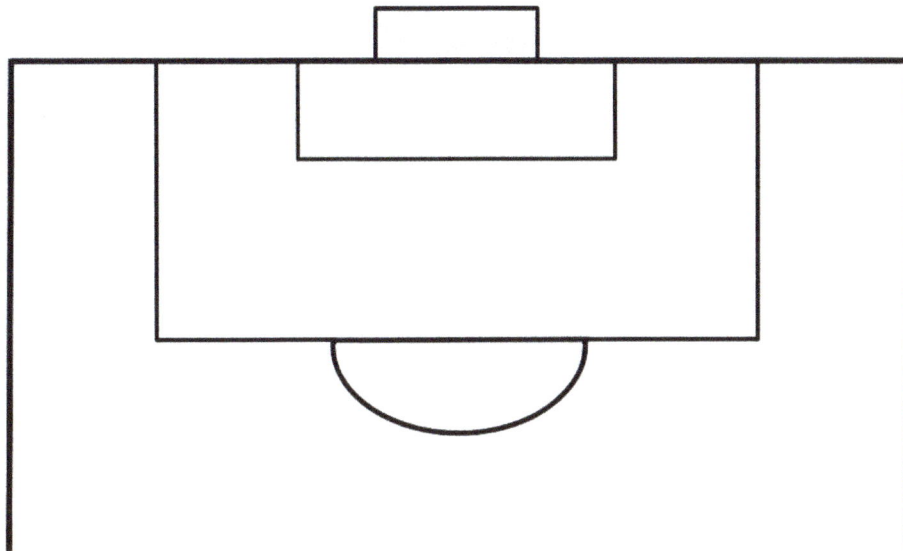

Practice	Key Technical Points

Notes for Next Time
(What went well, what you'd change)

Session Name:

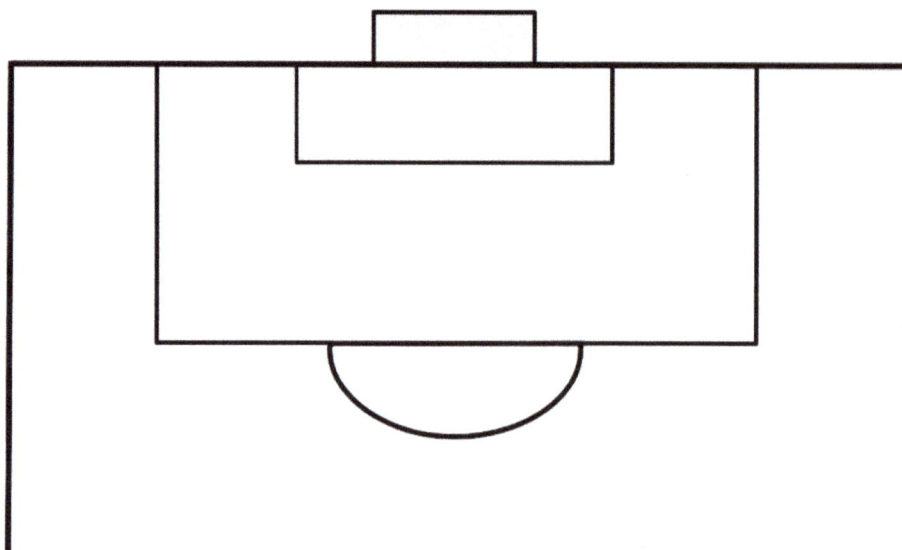

Practice	Key Technical Points

Notes for Next Time
(What went well, what you'd change)

Session Name:

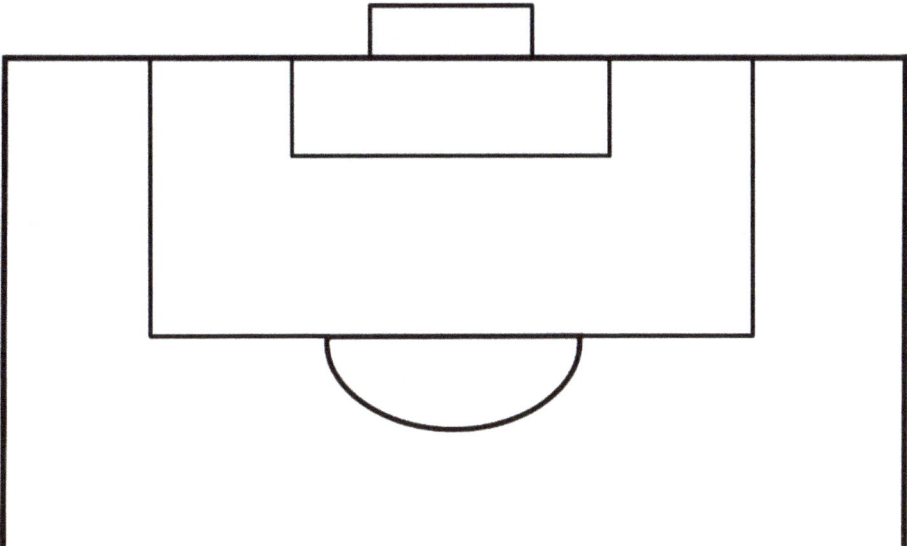

Practice	Key Technical Points

Notes for Next Time
(What went well, what you'd change)

Session Name:

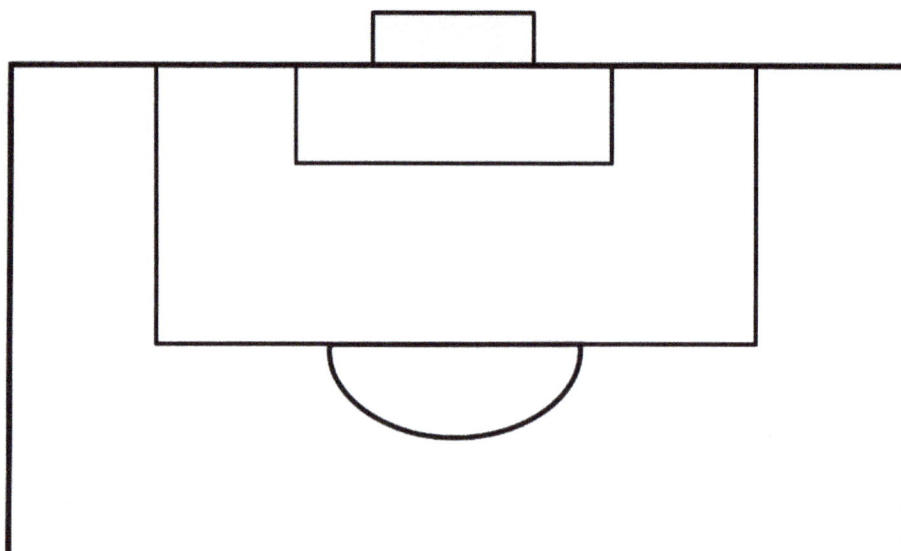

Practice	Key Technical Points

Notes for Next Time
(What went well, what you'd change)

Session Name:

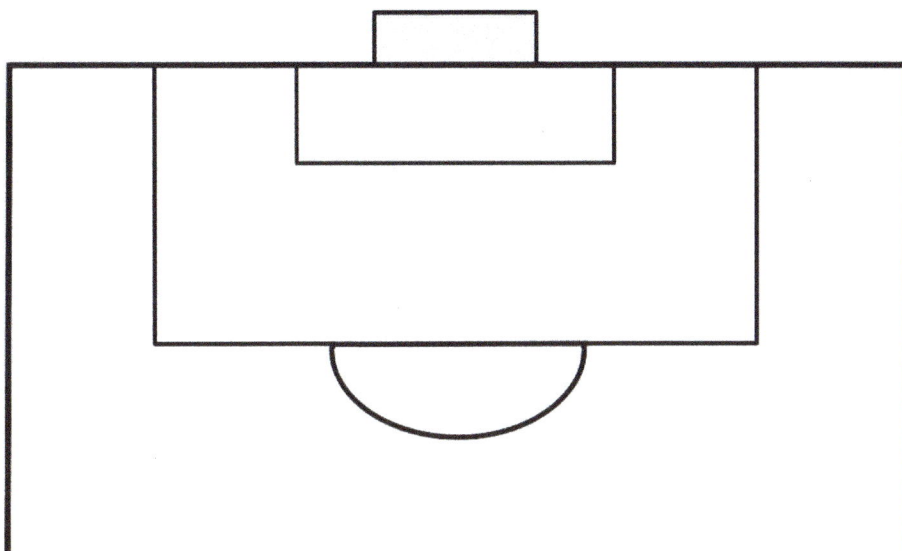

Practice	Key Technical Points

Notes for Next Time
(What went well, what you'd change)

Session Name:

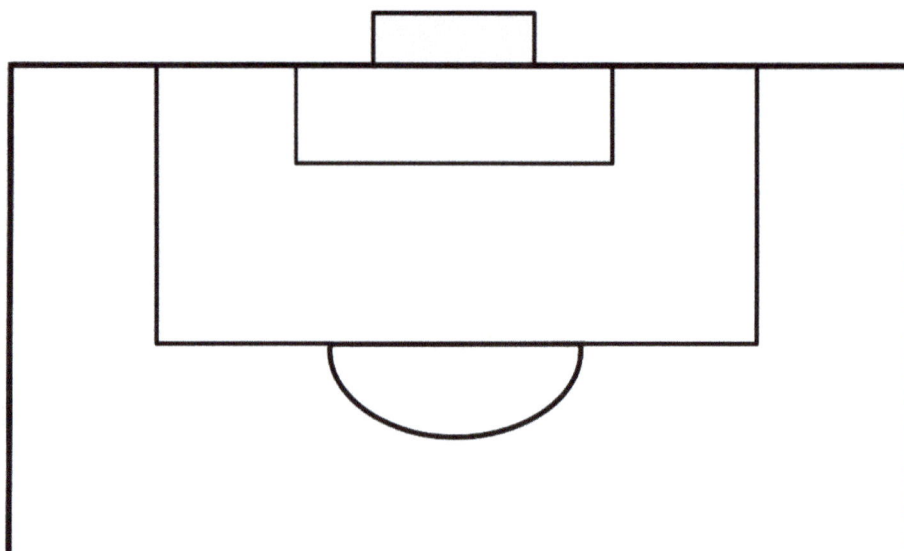

Practice	Key Technical Points

Notes for Next Time
(What went well, what you'd change)

Other Coaching Books from Bennion Kearny

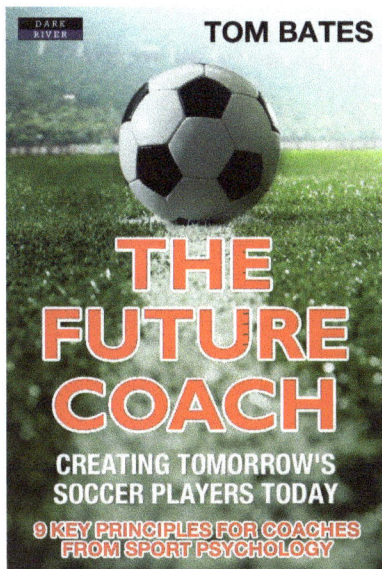

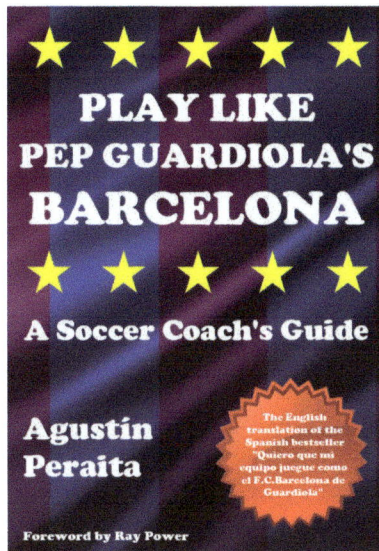

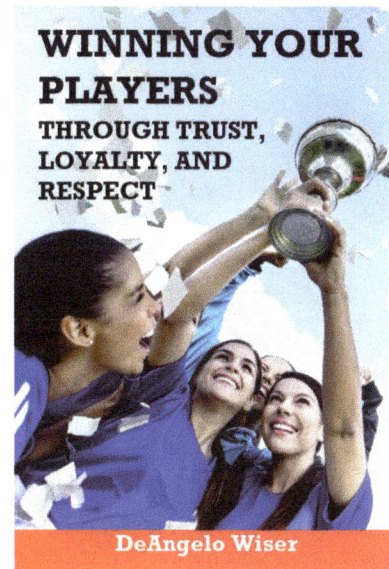

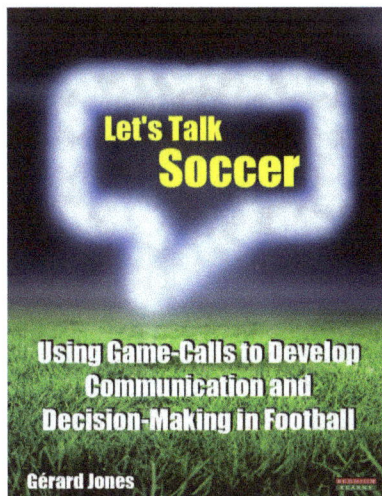

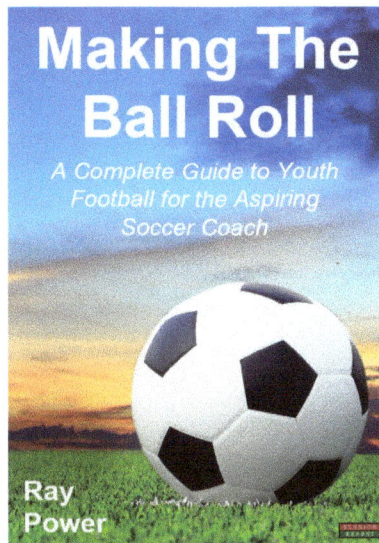

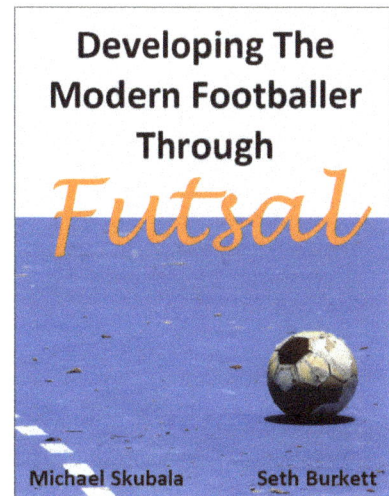

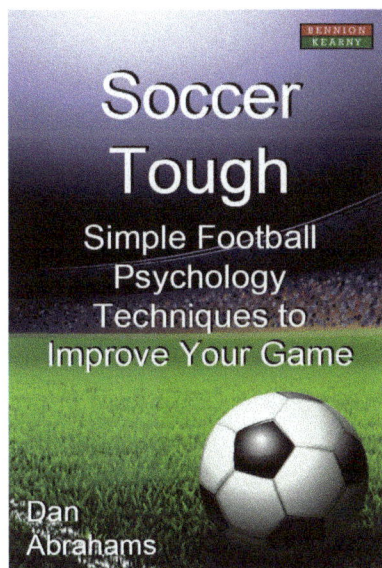

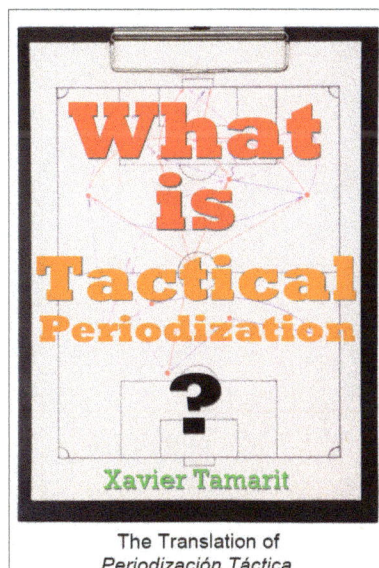

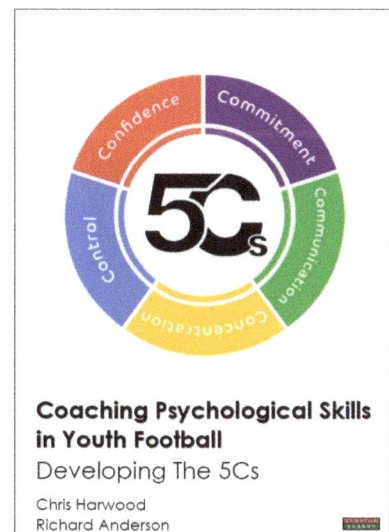

TOM BATES

DARK RIVER

THE FUTURE COACH

CREATING TOMORROW'S SOCCER PLAYERS TODAY

9 KEY PRINCIPLES FOR COACHES FROM SPORT PSYCHOLOGY

★ ★ ★ ★ ★

PLAY LIKE PEP GUARDIOLA'S BARCELONA

★ ★ ★ ★ ★

A Soccer Coach's Guide

Agustín Peraita

The English translation of the Spanish bestseller "Quiero que mi equipo juegue como el F.C.Barcelona de Guardiola"

Foreword by Ray Power

WINNING YOUR PLAYERS
THROUGH TRUST, LOYALTY, AND RESPECT

DeAngelo Wiser

Let's Talk **Soccer**

Using Game-Calls to Develop Communication and Decision-Making in Football

Gérard Jones

Making The Ball Roll

A Complete Guide to Youth Football for the Aspiring Soccer Coach

Ray Power

Developing The Modern Footballer Through *Futsal*

Michael Skubala   Seth Burkett

BENNION KEARNY

Soccer Tough

Simple Football Psychology Techniques to Improve Your Game

Dan Abrahams

What is Tactical Periodization
?

Xavier Tamarit

The Translation of *Periodización Táctica*

Confidence Commitment
Control **5Cs** Communication
Concentration

Coaching Psychological Skills in Youth Football

Developing The 5Cs

Chris Harwood
Richard Anderson

BENNION KEARNY

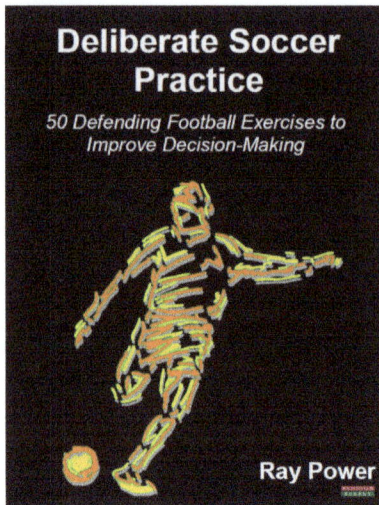

Deliberate Soccer Practice

50 Defending Football Exercises to Improve Decision-Making

Ray Power

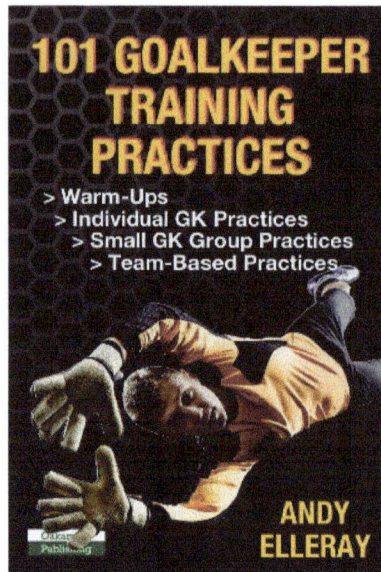

101 GOALKEEPER TRAINING PRACTICES

> Warm-Ups
> Individual GK Practices
> Small GK Group Practices
> Team-Based Practices

ANDY ELLERAY

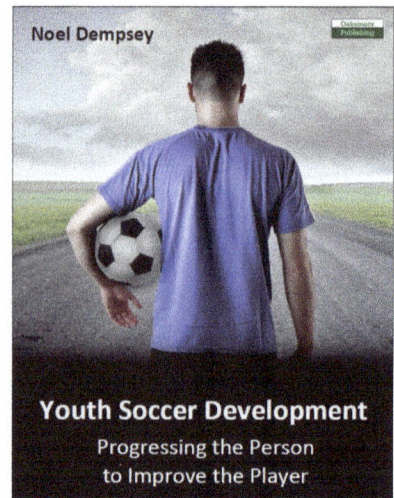

Noel Dempsey

Youth Soccer Development

Progressing the Person to Improve the Player

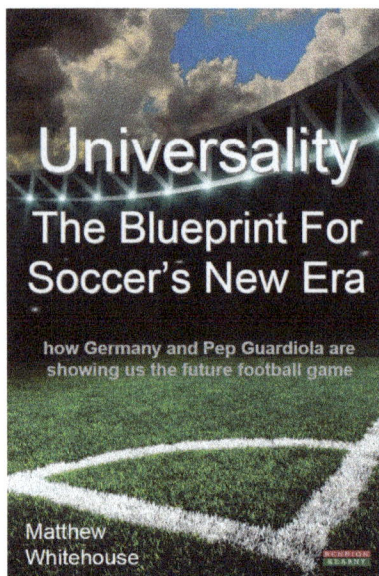

Universality
The Blueprint For Soccer's New Era

how Germany and Pep Guardiola are showing us the future football game

Matthew Whitehouse

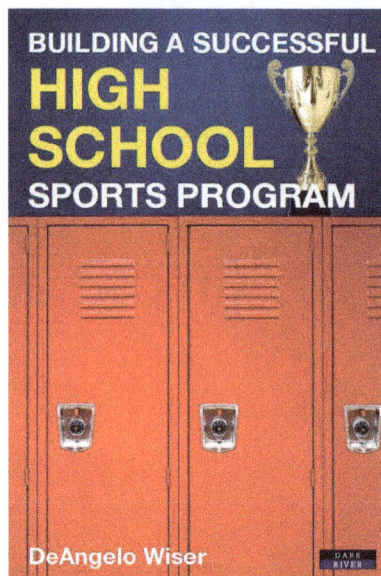

BUILDING A SUCCESSFUL HIGH SCHOOL SPORTS PROGRAM

DeAngelo Wiser

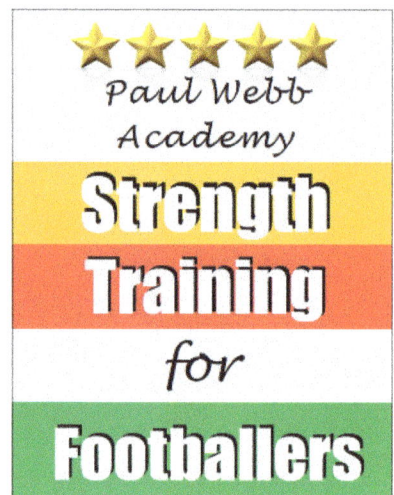

★★★★★

Paul Webb Academy

Strength Training *for* Footballers

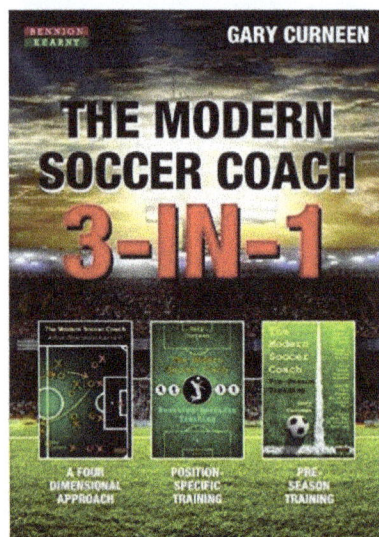

GARY CURNEEN

THE MODERN SOCCER COACH 3-IN-1

A FOUR DIMENSIONAL APPROACH

POSITION-SPECIFIC TRAINING

PRE-SEASON TRAINING

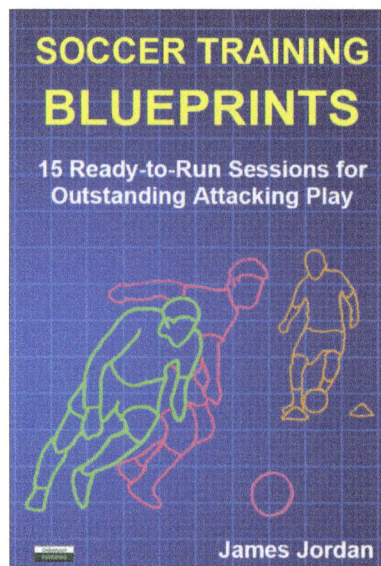

SOCCER TRAINING BLUEPRINTS

15 Ready-to-Run Sessions for Outstanding Attacking Play

James Jordan

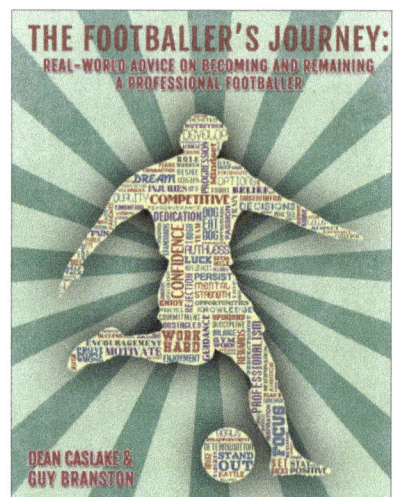

THE FOOTBALLER'S JOURNEY:
REAL-WORLD ADVICE ON BECOMING AND REMAINING A PROFESSIONAL FOOTBALLER

DEAN CASLAKE & GUY BRANSTON